The Constitution of the
State of South Dakota:
A Quick Reference Guide

Bootblack Budget Books
Copyright 2018 ©
ISBN-13: 978-1722233716
ISBN-10: 1722233710

Contents:

Article II: Division of The Powers of Government – Page 39

Section 1. Division of the Powers of Government

Article V: Judicial Department – Page 57

Article VI: Bill of Rights – Page 62

Article VII: Elections and Right of Suffrage – Page 72

Section 1. Right to Vote

Section 2. Voter Qualification

Section 3. Elections

Section 4 to 10. Superseded

Article VIII: Education and School Lands – Page 73

Article X: Municipal Corporations – Page 83

Repealed

Article XI: Revenue and Finance – Page 84

Article XIII: Public Indebtedness – Page 92

Article XIV: State Institutions – Page 105

Article XV: Militia – Page 107

Article XVI: Impeachment and
Removal From office – Page 109

Section 1. Power of Impeachment in House - Majority Required

Section 2. Trial of Impeachments - Presiding Officer

Section 3. Officers Subject to Impeachment - Grounds - Removal from Office - Criminal Prosecution

Section 4. Removals of Officers not Subject to Impeachment

Section 5. Suspension of Duties Between Impeachment and Acquittal

Section 6. Lieutenant Governor not to Try Governor

Section 7. Service of Copy of Impeachment Before Trial Required

Section 8. Impeachment Twice for Same Offense Prohibited

Article XVII: Corporations – Page 111

Section 1. Special Corporation Laws Prohibited – State-Controlled Corporations Excepted

Section 2. Invalidation of Charters Without Bona Fide Organization and Business

Section 3. Laws for Benefit of Corporation as Conditioned On Compliance With Constitutional Provision

Section 4. Corporations Subject to Eminent Domain – Police Power

Section 5. Casting of Votes for Directors or Managers

Section 6. Place of Business and Authorized Agent Required of Foreign Corporation

Section 7. Business to be Expressed in Charter – Real Estate Restricted

Section 8. Stocks and Bonds – Indebtedness Increase

Section 9. Legislature's Power to Alter, Revise, or Annul Corporate Charters – Creation, Renewal, or Extension

Section 10. Local Consent Required for Grant of Street Railroad Right

Section 11. Construction and Maintenance of Telegraph Lines – Controlling Interest in Competing Company Prohibited

Section 12. Railroad Corporations

Section 13. Movable Property of Railroad Corporation Considered Personalty – Execution and Sale

Section 14. Consolidation of Railroad Lines – Forfeiture of Charter for Evasion of Provisions

Section 15. Railways and Rail Companies Declared Public Highways and Common Carriers – Regulation of Rates

Section 16. Right to Construct and Operate Railroad – Passengers, Tonnage, and Cars

Section 17. Rate Discrimination Prevention

Section 18. Compensation for Private Property Taken for Public Use – Assessment of Damages

Section 19. Corporations Defined

Section 20. Monopolies and Trusts Prohibited – Combinations in Restraint of Trade – Legislative Powers

Section 21. Corporate or Syndicate Farming Prohibited – Definitions – Restrictions

Section 22. Restrictions – Application

Section 23. Loss of Qualification – Re-Qualification or Dissolution

Section 24. Annual Report – Violations – Action and Enforcement

Article XVIII: Banking and Currency – Page 122

Section 1. General Banking Law – Provisions Required

Section 2. Bank to Cease Operations Within Twenty Years of Organization – Reorganization

Section 3. Liability of Banking Corporation Shareholders and Stockholders – Exemption Under Federal Law

Article XIX: Congressional and Legislative Apportionment – Page 124

Section 1. Congressional Representatives Elected at Large

Section 2. Senatorial and Representative Districts – Apportionment

Article XXI: Miscellaneous – Page 126

Article XXII: Compact with the United States – Page 129

Section 1. Compact with the United States

Article XXIII: Amendments and Revisions of the Constitution – Page 131

Section 1. Amendments

Section 2. Revision

Section 3. Ratification

Article XXIV: Prohibition – Page 132

Repealed

Article XXV: Minority Representation – Page 133

Rejected

Section 14. Election of Two United States Senators – Two Representatives

Section 15. Adjournment After Election of Senators – Next Meeting

Section 16. Authorized Powers Only Pending Admission of State Into Union

Section 17. Validity of Ordinances and Schedule

Section 18. Freedom of Religion--Public Lands – Indian Lands – Uniformity of Taxation – Territorial Debt – Public Schools – Federal Reservations--Irrevocability

Section 19. Tenure of Elected Officers

Section 20. Time of General Election

Section 21. Form of Ballot

Section 22. Enrollment of Constitution--Delivery to Secretary of State – Inclusion In State Laws – Copy to President of United States

Section 23. Agreement by Joint Commission Concerning Territorial Records, Books, and Archives.

Article XXVII: State Control of Manufacture and Sale of Liquor – Page 149

Repealed

Article XXVIII: County Investment of Permanent School and Endowment Funds – Page 150

Section 1. School and Governmental Bonds – Farm Loans

Article XXIX: State Elevators, Warehouses, Flouring Mills, and Packing Houses – Page 151

Section 1. Provision for elevators and warehouses--Marketing of agricultural products--Flouring mills and packing houses

PREAMBLE

We, the people of South Dakota, grateful to Almighty God for our civil and religious liberties, in order to form a more perfect and independent government, establish justice, insure tranquility, provide for the common defense, promote the general welfare and preserve to ourselves and to our posterity the blessings of liberty, do ordain and establish this Constitution for the state of South Dakota.

ARTICLE I: NAME AND BOUNDARY

Section 1. Name of State

The name of the state shall be South Dakota.

Section 2. Boundaries of State

The boundaries of the state of South Dakota shall be as follows: Beginning at the point of intersection of the western boundary line of the state of Minnesota, with the northern boundary line of the state of Iowa and running thence northerly along the western boundary line of the state of Minnesota, to its intersection with the seventh standard parallel; thence west on the line of the seventh standard parallel produced due west to its intersection with the twenty-seventh meridian of longitude west from Washington; thence south on the twenty-seventh meridian of longitude west from Washington to its intersection with the northern boundary line of the state of Nebraska; thence easterly along the northern boundary line of the state of Nebraska to its intersection with the western boundary line of the state of Iowa; thence northerly along the western boundary line of the state of Iowa to its intersection with the northern boundary line of the state of Iowa; thence east along the northern boundary line of the state of Iowa to the place of beginning.

ARTICLE II: DIVISION OF THE POWERS OF GOVERNMENT

The powers of the government of the state are divided into three distinct departments, the legislative, executive and judicial; and the powers and duties of each are prescribed by this Constitution.

ARTICLE III: LEGISLATIVE DEPARTMENT

Section 1. Legislative power – Initiative and Referendum

The legislative power of the state shall be vested in a Legislature which shall consist of a senate and House of Representatives. However, the people expressly reserve to themselves the right to propose measures, which shall be submitted to a vote of the electors of the state, and also the right to require that any laws which the Legislature may have enacted shall be submitted to a vote of the electors of the state before going into effect, except such laws as may be necessary for the immediate preservation of the public peace, health or safety, support of the state government and its existing public institutions. Not more than five per cent of the qualified electors of the state shall be required to invoke either the initiative or the referendum. This section shall not be construed so as to deprive the Legislature or any member thereof of the right to propose any measure. The veto power of the Executive shall not be exercised as to measures referred to a vote of the people. This section shall apply to municipalities. The enacting clause of all laws approved by vote of the electors of the state shall be: "Be it enacted by the people of South Dakota." The Legislature shall make suitable provisions for carrying into effect the provisions of this section.

Section 2. Number of legislators – Regular Sessions

After the Legislature elected for the years 1937 and 1938 the number of members of the House of Representatives shall not be less than fifty nor more than seventy-five and the number of members of the senate shall not be less than twenty-five nor more than thirty-five. The sessions of the Legislature shall be biennial except as otherwise provided in this Constitution.

Section 3. Qualifications for Legislative Office – Officers Ineligible

No person is eligible for the office of senator who is not a qualified elector in the district from which such person is chosen, a citizen of the United States, and who has not attained the age of twenty-one years, and who has not been a resident of the state for two years next preceding election. No person is eligible for the office of representative who is not a qualified elector in the district from which such person is chosen, and a citizen of the United States, and who has not been a resident of the state for two years next preceding election, and who has not attained the age of twenty-one years. No judge or clerk of any court, secretary of state, attorney general, state's attorney, recorder, sheriff or collector of public moneys, member of either house of Congress, or person holding any lucrative office under the United States, or this state, or any foreign government, shall be a member of the Legislature: provided, that appointments in the militia, the offices of notary public and justice of the peace shall not be considered lucrative; nor shall any person holding any office of honor or profit under any foreign government or under the government of the United States, except postmasters whose annual compensation does not exceed the sum of three hundred dollars, hold any office in either branch of the Legislature or become a member thereof.

Section 4. Disqualification for Conviction of Crime – Defaults on Public Money

No person who has been, or hereafter shall be, convicted of bribery, perjury, or other infamous crime, nor any person who has been, or may be collector or holder of public moneys, who shall not have accounted for and paid over, according to law, all such moneys due from him, shall be eligible to the Legislature or to any office in either branch thereof.

Section 5. Legislative Reapportionment

The Legislature shall apportion its membership by dividing the state into as many single-member, legislative districts as there are state senators. House districts shall be established wholly within senatorial districts and shall be either single-member or dual-member districts as the Legislature shall determine. Legislative districts shall consist of compact, contiguous territory and shall have population as nearly equal as is practicable, based on the last preceding federal census. An apportionment shall be made by the Legislature in 1983 and in 1991, and every ten years after 1991. Such apportionment shall be accomplished by December first of the year in which the apportionment is required. If any Legislature whose duty it is to make an apportionment shall fail to make the same as herein provided, it shall be the duty of the Supreme Court within ninety days to make such apportionment.

Section 6. Legislative Terms of Office – Compensation – Regular Sessions

The terms of office of the members of the Legislature shall be two years; they shall receive for their services the salary fixed by law under the provisions of Section 2 of article XXI of this Constitution, and five cents for every mile of necessary travel in going to and returning from the place of meeting of the Legislature on the most usual route. No person may serve more than four consecutive terms or a total of eight consecutive years in the senate and more than four consecutive terms or a total of eight consecutive years in the House of Representatives. However, this restriction does not apply to partial terms to which a legislator may be appointed. A regular session of the Legislature shall be held each year and shall not exceed forty legislative days; excluding Sundays, holidays and legislative recess, except in cases of impeachment, and members of the Legislature shall receive no other pay or perquisites except salary and mileage.

Section 7. Convening of Annual Sessions

The Legislature shall meet at the seat of government on the second Tuesday of January at 12 o'clock pm. and at no other time except as provided by this Constitution.

Section 8. Oath Required of Legislators and Officers – Forfeiture of Office for False Swearing

Members of the Legislature and officers thereof, before they enter upon their official duties, shall take and subscribe the following oath or affirmation: I do solemnly swear (or affirm) that I will support the Constitution of the United States and the Constitution of the state of South Dakota, and will faithfully discharge the duties of (senator, representative or officer) according to the best of my abilities, and that I have not knowingly or intentionally paid or contributed anything, or made any promise in the nature of a bribe, to directly or indirectly influence any vote at the election at which I was chosen to fill said office, and have not accepted, nor will I accept or receive directly or indirectly, any money, pass, or any other valuable thing, from any corporation, company or person, for any vote or influence I may give or withhold on any bill or resolution, or appropriation, or for any other official act. This oath shall be administered by a judge of the Supreme or circuit Court, or the presiding officer of either house, in the hall of the house to which the member or officer is elected, and the secretary of state shall record and file the oath subscribed by each member and officer. Any member or officer of the Legislature who shall refuse to take the oath herein prescribed shall forfeit his office. Any member or officer of the Legislature who shall be convicted of having sworn falsely to, or violated his said oath, shall forfeit his office and be disqualified thereafter from holding the office of senator or member of the house of representatives or any office within the gift of the Legislature.

Section 9. Each House as Judge of Qualifications – Quorum – Rules of Proceedings – Officers and Employees

Each house shall be the judge of the election returns and qualifications of its own members. A majority of the members of each house shall constitute a quorum, but a smaller number may adjourn from day-to-day, and may compel the attendance of absent members in such a manner and under such penalty as each house may provide. Each house shall determine the rules of its proceedings, shall choose its own officers and employees and fix the pay thereof, except as otherwise provided in this Constitution.

Section 10. Filling Legislative Vacancies

The Governor shall make appointments to fill such vacancies as may occur in either house of the Legislature

Section 11. Legislators' Privilege From Arrest – Freedom of Debate

Senators and representatives shall, in all cases except treason, felony or breach of the peace, be privileged from arrest during the session of the Legislature, and in going to and returning from the same; and for words used in any speech or debate in either house; they shall not be questioned in any other place.

Section 12. Legislators Ineligible for Other Office – Contracts with State or County

No member of the Legislature shall, during the term for which he was elected, be appointed or elected to any civil office in the state which shall have been created, or the emoluments of which shall have been increased during the term for which he was elected, nor shall any member receive any civil appointment from the Governor, the Governor and senate, or from the Legislature during the term for which he shall have been elected, and all such appointments and all votes given for any such members for any such office or appointment shall be void; nor shall any member of the Legislature during the term for which he shall have been elected, or within one year thereafter, be interested, directly or indirectly, in any contract with the state or any county thereof, authorized by any law passed during the term for which he shall have been elected.

Section 13. Legislative Journals – Recording of Yeas and Nays

Each house shall keep a journal of its proceedings and publish the same from time to time, except such parts as require secrecy, and the yeas and nays of members on any question shall be taken at the desire of one-sixth of those present and entered upon the journal.

Section 14. Elections Viva Voce

In all elections to be made by the Legislature the members thereof shall vote viva voce and their votes shall be entered in the journal.

Section 15. Open Legislative Sessions – Exception

The sessions of each house and of the committee of the whole shall be open, unless when the business is such as ought to be kept secret.

Section 16. Adjournment of Legislative Houses

Neither house shall without the consent of the other adjourn for more than three days, nor to any other place than that in which the two houses shall be sitting.

Section 17. Reading of Bills

Every bill shall be read twice, by number and title once when introduced, and once upon final passage, but one reading at length may be demanded at any time before final passage.

Section 18. Enacting Clause – Assent by Majority – Recording of Votes

The enacting clause of a law shall be: "Be it enacted by the Legislature of the State of South Dakota" and no law shall be passed unless by assent of a majority of all the members elected to each house of the Legislature. And the question upon the final passage shall be taken upon its last reading, and the yeas and nays shall be entered upon the journal.

Section 19. Signing of Bills and Resolutions

The presiding officer of each house shall, in the presence of the house over which he presides, sign all bills and joint resolutions passed by the Legislature, after their titles have been publicly read immediately before signing, and the fact of signing shall be entered upon the journal.

Section 20. Origin of Bills – Amendment in other House

Any bill may originate in either house of the Legislature, and a bill passed by one house may be amended in the other.

Section 21. One Subject Expressed in Title

No law shall embrace more than one subject, which shall be expressed in its title.

Section 22. Effective Date of Acts – Emergency Clause

No act shall take effect until ninety days after the adjournment of the session at which it passed, unless in case of emergency, (to be expressed in the preamble or body of the act) the Legislature shall by a vote of two-thirds of all the members elected of each house, otherwise direct.

Section 23. Private and Special Laws Prohibited

The Legislature is prohibited from enacting any private or special laws in the following cases:

1. Granting divorces.

2. Changing the names of persons or places, or constituting one person the heir at law of another.

3. Locating or changing county seats.

4. Regulating county and township affairs.

5. Incorporating cities, towns and villages or changing or amending the charter of any town, city or village, or laying out, opening, vacating or altering town plats, streets, wards, alleys and public ground.

6. Providing for sale or mortgage of real estate belonging to minors or others under disability.

7. Authorizing persons to keep ferries across streams wholly within the state.

8. Remitting fines, penalties or forfeitures.

9. Granting to an individual, association or corporation any special or exclusive privilege, immunity or franchise whatever.

10. Providing for the management of common schools.

11. Creating, increasing or decreasing fees, percentages or allowances of public officers during the term for which said officers are elected or appointed. But the Legislature may repeal any existing special law relating to the foregoing subdivisions. In all other cases where a general law can be applicable no special law shall be enacted.

Section 24. Release of debt to State or Municipality

The Legislature shall have no power to release or extinguish, in whole or in part, the indebtedness, liability or obligation of any corporation or individual to this state or to any municipal corporation therein.

Section 25. Games of Chance Prohibited – Exceptions

The Legislature shall not authorize any game of chance, lottery, or gift enterprise, under any pretense, or for any purpose whatever provided, however, it shall be lawful for the Legislature to authorize by law, bona fide veterans, charitable, educational, religious or fraternal organizations, civic and service clubs, volunteer fire departments, or such other public spirited organizations as it may recognize, to conduct games of chance when the entire net proceeds of such games of chance are to be devoted to educational, charitable, patriotic, religious, or other public spirited uses. However, it shall be lawful for the Legislature to authorize by law a state lottery or video games of chance, or both, which are regulated by the state of South Dakota, either separately by the state or jointly with one or more states, and which are owned and operated by the state of South Dakota, either separately by the state or jointly with one or more states or persons, provided any such video games of chance shall not directly dispense coins or tokens. However, the Legislature shall not expand the statutory authority existing as of June 1, 1994, regarding any private ownership of state lottery games or video games of chance, or both. The Legislature shall establish the portion of proceeds due the state from such lottery or video games of chance, or both, and the purposes for which those proceeds are to be used. SDCL 42-7A, and its amendments, regulations, and related laws, and all acts and contracts relying for authority upon such laws and regulations, beginning July 1, 1987, to the effective date of this amendment, are ratified and approved. Further, it shall be lawful for the Legislature to authorize by law, limited card games and slot machines within the city limits of Deadwood, provided that 60% of the voters of the City of Deadwood approve legislatively authorized card games and slot machines at an election called for such purpose. The entire net Municipal proceeds of such card games and slot machines shall be devoted to the Historic Restoration and Preservation of Deadwood.

Section 26. Municipal Powers Denied to Private Organizations

The Legislature shall not delegate to any special commission, private corporation or association, any power to make, supervise or interfere with any municipal improvement, money, property, effects, whether held in trust or otherwise, or levy taxes, or to select a capital site, or to perform any municipal functions whatever.

Section 27. Suits Against the State

The Legislature shall direct by law in what manner and in what courts suits may be brought against the state.

Section 28. Bribery and Corrupt Solicitation of Officers – Compelling Testimony – Immunity from Prosecution

Any person who shall give, demand, offer, directly or indirectly, any money, testimonial, privilege or personal advantage, thing of value to any executive or judicial officer or member of the Legislature, to influence him in the performance of any of his official or public duties, shall be guilty of bribery and shall be punished in such manner as shall be provided by law. The offense of corrupt solicitation of members of the Legislature, or of public officers of the state, or any municipal division thereof, and any effort towards solicitation of said members of the Legislature, or officers to influence their official actions shall be defined by law, and shall be punishable by fine and imprisonment. Any person may be compelled to testify in investigation or judicial proceedings against any person charged with having committed any offense of bribery or corrupt solicitation, and shall not be permitted to withhold his testimony upon the ground that it may criminate himself, but said testimony shall not afterwards be used against him in any judicial proceeding except for bribery in giving such testimony, and any person convicted of either of the offenses aforesaid shall be disqualified from holding any office or position or office of trust or profit in this state.

Section 29. Legislative Powers in Emergency from Enemy Attack

Notwithstanding any general or special provisions of the Constitution, in order to insure continuity of state and local governmental operations in periods of emergency resulting from disasters caused by enemy attack, the Legislature shall have the power and the immediate duty (1) to provide for prompt and temporary succession to the powers and duties of public offices, of whatever nature and whether filled by election or appointment, the incumbents of which may become unavailable for carrying on the powers and duties of such offices, and (2) to adopt such other measures as may be necessary and proper for insuring the continuity of governmental operations. In the exercise of the powers hereby conferred the Legislature shall in all respects conform to the requirements of this Constitution except to the extent that in the judgment of the Legislature so to do would be impracticable or would admit of undue delay.

Section 30. Power of Committee of Legislature to Suspend Administrative Rules and Regulations

The Legislature may by law empower a committee comprised of members of both houses of the Legislature, acting during recesses or between sessions, to suspend rules and regulations promulgated by any administrative department or agency from going into effect until July 1 after the Legislature reconvenes.

Section 31. Convening of Special Sessions upon Petition

In addition to the provisions of Article IV, Section 3, the Legislature shall be convened in special session by the presiding officers of both houses upon the written petition of two-thirds of the members of each house. The petition shall state the purposes of the session, and only business encompassed by those purposes may be transacted.

Section 32. Term Limitations for United States Congressmen

Commencing with the 1992 election, no person may be elected to more than two consecutive terms in the United States senate or more than six consecutive terms in the United States House of Representatives.

ARTICLE IV: EXECUTIVE DEPARTMENT

Section 1. Executive Power

The executive power of the state is vested in the Governor.

Section 2. Qualification, Election and Term

The Governor and lieutenant governor must be citizens of the United States, have attained the age of twenty-one years, and be residents of the State of South Dakota for two years preceding their election. They shall be jointly elected for a term of four years at a general election held in a non-presidential election year. The candidates having the highest number of votes cast jointly for them shall be elected. Commencing with the 1974 general election, no person shall be elected to more than two consecutive terms as Governor or as lieutenant governor. The election procedure shall be as prescribed by law.

Section 3. Powers and Duties of the Governor

The Governor shall be responsible for the faithful execution of the law. He may, by appropriate action or proceeding brought in the name of the state, enforce compliance with any constitutional or legislative mandate, or restrain violation of any constitutional or legislative power, duty or right by any officer, department or agency of the state or any of its civil divisions. This authority shall not authorize any action or proceedings against the Legislature. He shall be commander-in-chief of the armed forces of the state, except when they shall be called into the service of the United States, and may call them out to execute the laws, to preserve order, to suppress insurrection or to repel invasion. The Governor shall commission all officers of the state. He may at any time require information, in writing or otherwise, from the officers of any administrative department, office or agency upon any subject relating to the respective offices. The Governor shall at the beginning of each session, and may at other times, give the Legislature information concerning the affairs of the state and recommend the measures he considers necessary. The Governor may convene the Legislature or either house thereof alone in special session by a proclamation stating the purposes of the session, and only business encompassed by such purposes shall be transacted. Whenever a vacancy occurs in any office and no provision is made by the Constitution or laws for filling such vacancy, the Governor shall have the power to fill such vacancy by appointment. The Governor may, except as to convictions on impeachment, grant pardons, commutations, and reprieves, and may suspend and remit fines and forfeitures.

Section 4. Veto Power

Whenever the Legislature is in session, any bill presented to the Governor for signature shall become law when the Governor signs the bill or fails to veto the bill within five days, not including Saturdays, Sundays, or holidays, of presentation. A vetoed bill shall be returned by the Governor to the Legislature together with the Governor's objections within five days, not including Saturdays, Sundays, or holidays, of presentation if the Legislature is in session or upon the reconvening of the Legislature from a recess. Any vetoed bill shall be reconsidered by the Legislature and, if two-thirds of all members of each house shall pass the bill, it shall become law.   Whenever a bill has been presented to the Governor and the Legislature has adjourned sine die or recessed for more than five days within five days from presentation, the bill shall become law when the Governor signs the bill or fails to veto it within fifteen days after such adjournment or start of the recess.   The Governor may strike any items of any bill passed by the Legislature making appropriations. The procedure for reconsidering items struck by the Governor shall be the same as is prescribed for the passage of bills over the executive veto. All items not struck shall become law as provided herein.   Bills with errors in style or form may be returned to the Legislature by the Governor with specific recommendations for change. Bills returned shall be treated in the same manner as vetoed bills except that specific recommendations for change as to style or form may be approved by a majority vote of all the members of each house. If the Governor certifies that the bill conforms to the Governor's specific recommendations, the bill shall become law. If the Governor fails to certify the bill, it shall be returned to the Legislature as a vetoed bill.

Section 5. Powers and Duties of Lieutenant Governor

The lieutenant governor shall be president of the senate but shall have no vote unless the senators are equally divided. The lieutenant governor shall perform the duties and exercise the powers that may be delegated to him by the Governor.

Section 6. Succession of Executive Power

When the office of Governor shall become vacant through death, resignation, failure to qualify, conviction after impeachment or permanent disability of the Governor, the lieutenant governor shall succeed to the office and powers of the Governor. When the Governor is unable to serve by reason of continuous absence from the state, or other temporary disability, the executive power shall devolve upon the lieutenant governor for the residue of the term or until the disability is removed. Whenever there is a permanent vacancy in the office of the lieutenant governor, the Governor shall nominate a lieutenant governor who shall take office upon confirmation by a majority vote of all the members of each house of the Legislature.

Whenever there is a concurrent vacancy in the office of Governor and lieutenant governor, the order of succession for the office of Governor shall be as provided by law. The Supreme Court shall have original and exclusive jurisdiction to determine when a continuous absence from the state or disability has occurred in the office of the Governor or a permanent vacancy exists in the office of lieutenant governor.

Section 7. Other Executive Officers – Powers, Duties, and Term Limitations

There shall be chosen by the qualified electors of the state at the general election of the Governor and every four years thereafter the following constitutional officers: attorney general, secretary of state, auditor, treasurer, and commissioner of school and public lands, who shall severally hold their offices for a term of four years. Commencing with the 1992 general election, no person may be elected to more than two consecutive terms as attorney general, secretary of state, auditor, treasurer, or commissioner of school and public lands.

Section 8. Reorganization

All executive and administrative offices, boards, agencies, commissions and instrumentalities of the state government and their respective functions, powers and duties, except for the office of Governor, lieutenant governor, attorney general, secretary of state, auditor, treasurer, and commissioner of school and public lands, shall be allocated by law among and within not more than twenty-five principal departments, organized as far as practicable according to major purposes, by no later than July 1, 1974. Subsequently, all new powers or functions shall be assigned to administrative offices, agencies and instrumentalities in such manner as will tend to provide an orderly arrangement in the administrative organization of state government. Temporary commissions may be established by law and need not be allocated within a principal department. Except as to elected constitutional officers, the Governor may make such changes in the organization of offices, boards, commissions, agencies and instrumentalities, and in allocation of their functions, powers and duties, as he considers necessary for efficient administration. If such changes affect existing law, they shall be set forth in executive orders, which shall be submitted to the Legislature within five legislative days after it convenes, and shall become effective, and shall have the force of law, within ninety days after submission, unless disapproved by a resolution concurred in by a majority of all the members of either house.

Section 9. Appointment and Removal Power

Each principal department shall be under the supervision of the Governor and, unless otherwise provided in this Constitution or by law, shall be headed by a single executive. Such single executive, unless provided otherwise by the Constitution, shall be nominated and, by and with the advice and consent of the senate, appointed by the Governor and shall hold office for a term to expire at the end of the term for which the Governor was elected, unless sooner removed by the Governor. Except as otherwise provided in this Constitution, whenever a board, commission or other body shall head a principal department of the state government, the members thereof shall be nominated and, by and with the advice and consent of the senate, appointed by the Governor. The term of office and removal of such members shall be as prescribed by law. The Governor shall have power to nominate and make interim appointments requiring senate confirmation during recess of the Legislature except that such nominations and interim appointments shall extend only to the end of the Governor's term or until acted upon by the Legislature. Section Section 10 to 13. Superseded.

ARTICLE V: JUDICIAL DEPARTMENT

Section 1. Judicial powers. The judicial power of the state is vested in a unified judicial system consisting of a Supreme Court, circuit courts of general jurisdiction and courts of limited original jurisdiction as established by the Legislature.

Section 2. Supreme Court

The Supreme Court is the highest court of the state. It consists of a chief justice and four associate justices. Upon request by the Supreme Court the Legislature may increase the number of justices to seven. All justices shall be selected from compact districts established by the Legislature, and each district shall have one justice.

Section 3. Circuit Courts

The circuit courts consist of such number of circuits and judges as the Supreme Court determines by rule.

Section 4. Courts of Limited Jurisdiction

Courts of limited jurisdiction consist of all courts created by the Legislature having limited original jurisdiction.

Section 5. Jurisdiction of Courts

The Supreme Court shall have such appellate jurisdiction as may be provided by the Legislature and the Supreme Court or any justice thereof may issue any original or remedial writ which shall then be heard and determined by that court. The Governor has authority to require opinions of the Supreme Court upon important questions of law involved in the exercise of his executive power and upon solemn occasions. The circuit courts have original jurisdiction in all cases except as to any limited original jurisdiction granted to other courts by the Legislature. The circuit courts and judges thereof have the power to issue, hear and determine all original and remedial writs. The circuit courts have such appellate jurisdiction as may be provided by law. Imposition or execution of a sentence may be suspended by the court empowered to impose the sentence unless otherwise provided by law.

Section 6. Qualifications of Judicial Personnel

Justices of the Supreme Court, judges of the circuit courts and persons presiding over courts of limited jurisdiction must be citizens of the United States, residents of the state of South Dakota and voting residents within the district, circuit or jurisdiction from which they are elected or appointed. No Supreme Court justice shall be deemed to have lost his voting residence in a district by reason of his removal to the seat of government in the discharge of his official duties. Justices of the Supreme Court and judges of circuit courts must be licensed to practice law in the state of South Dakota.

Section 7. Judicial Selection

Circuit court judges shall be elected in a nonpolitical election by the electorate of the circuit each represents for an eight-year term. A vacancy, as defined by law, in the office of a Supreme Court justice or circuit court judge, shall be filled by appointment of the Governor from one of two or more persons nominated by the judicial qualifications commission. The appointment to fill a vacancy of a circuit court judge shall be for the balance of the unexpired term; and the appointment to fill a vacancy of a Supreme Court justice shall be subject to approval or rejection as hereinafter set forth. Retention of each Supreme Court justice shall, in the manner provided by law, be subject to approval or rejection on a nonpolitical ballot at the first general election following the expiration of three years from the date of his appointment. Thereafter, each Supreme Court justice shall be subject to approval or rejection in like manner every eighth year. All incumbent Supreme Court justices at the time of the effective date of this amendment shall be subject to a retention election in the general election in the year in which their respective existing terms expire.

Section 8. Selection of the Chief Justice

The chief justice shall be selected from among the justices of the Supreme Court for a term and in a manner to be provided by law. The chief justice may resign his office without resigning from the Supreme Court.

Section 9. Qualifications Commission

The Legislature shall provide by law for the establishment of a judicial qualifications commission which have such powers as the Legislature may provide, including the power to investigate complaints against any justice or judge and to conduct confidential hearings concerning the removal or involuntary retirement of a justice or judge. The Supreme Court shall prescribe by rule the means to implement and enforce the powers of the commission. On recommendation of the judicial qualifications commission the Supreme Court, after hearing, may censure, remove or retire a justice or judge for action which constitutes willful misconduct in office, willful and persistent failure to perform his duties, habitual intemperance, disability that seriously interferes with the performance of the duties or conduct prejudicial to the administration of justice which brings a judicial office into disrepute. No justice or judge shall sit in judgment in any hearing involving his own removal or retirement.

Section 10. Restrictions

During his term of office no Supreme Court justice or circuit court judge shall engage in the practice of law. Any Supreme Court justice or circuit court judge who becomes a candidate for an elective non-judicial office shall there by forfeit his judicial office.

Section 11. Administration

The chief justice is the administrative head of the unified judicial system. The chief justice shall submit an annual consolidated budget for the entire unified judicial system, and the total cost of the system shall be paid by the state. The Legislature may provide by law for the reimbursement to the state of appropriate portions of such cost by governmental subdivisions. The Supreme Court shall appoint such court personnel as it deems necessary to serve at its pleasure. The chief justice shall appoint a presiding circuit judge for each judicial circuit to serve at the pleasure of the chief justice. Each presiding circuit judge shall have such administrative power as the Supreme Court designates by rule and may, unless it be otherwise provided by law, appoint judicial personnel to courts of limited jurisdiction to serve at his pleasure. Each presiding circuit judge shall appoint clerks and other court personnel for the counties in his circuit who shall serve at his pleasure at a compensation fixed by law. Duties of clerks shall be defined by Supreme Court rule. The chief justice shall have power to assign any circuit judge to sit on another circuit court, or on the Supreme Court in case of a vacancy or in place of a justice who is disqualified or unable to act. The chief justice may authorize a justice to sit as a judge in any circuit court. The chief justice may authorize retired justices and judges to perform any judicial duties to the extent provided by law and as directed by the Supreme Court.

Section 12. Rule-Making Power

The Supreme Court shall have general superintending powers over all courts and may make rules of practice and procedure and rules governing the administration of all courts. The Supreme Court by rule shall govern terms of courts, admission to the bar, and discipline of members of the bar. These rules may be changed by the Legislature.

Section 13. Transition

The Legislature by law and the Supreme Court by rule shall provide for the orderly transition of the judicial system in conformity with this article.

Section Section 14 to 39.

Superseded

ARTICLE VI: BILL OF RIGHTS

Section 1. Inherent rights. All men are born equally free and independent, and have certain inherent rights, among which are those of enjoying and defending life and liberty, of acquiring and protecting property and the pursuit of happiness. To secure these rights governments are instituted among men, deriving their just powers from the consent of the governed.

Section 2. Due Process – Right to Work

No person shall be deprived of life, liberty or property without due process of law. The right of persons to work shall not be denied or abridged on account of membership or non-membership in any labor union, or labor organization.

Section 3. Freedom of Religion – Support of Religion Prohibited

The right to worship God according to the dictates of conscience shall never be infringed. No person shall be denied any civil or political right, privilege or position on account of his religious opinions; but the liberty of conscience hereby secured shall not be so construed as to excuse licentiousness, the invasion of the rights of others, or justify practices inconsistent with the peace or safety of the state. No person shall be compelled to attend or support any ministry or place of worship against his consent nor shall any preference be given by law to any religious establishment or mode of worship. No money or property of the state shall be given or appropriated for the benefit of any sectarian or religious society or institution.

Section 4. Right of Petition and Peaceable Assembly

The right of petition, and of the people peaceably to assemble to consult for the common good and make known their opinions, shall never be abridged.

Section 5. Freedom of Speech – Truth as Defense – Jury Trial

Every person may freely speak, write and publish on all subjects, being responsible for the abuse of that right. In all trials for libel, both civil and criminal, the truth, when published with good motives and for justifiable ends, shall be a sufficient defense. The jury shall have the right to determine the fact and the law under the direction of the court.

Section 6. Jury Trial – Reduced Jury – Three-Fourths Vote

The right of trial by jury shall remain inviolate and shall extend to all cases at law without regard to the amount in controversy, but the Legislature may provide for a jury of less an twelve in any court not a court of record and for the decision of civil cases by three-fourths of the jury in any court.

Section 7. Rights of Accused

In all criminal prosecutions the accused shall have the right to defend in person and by counsel; to demand the nature and cause of the accusation against him; to have a copy thereof; to meet the witnesses against him face to face; to have compulsory process served for obtaining witnesses in his behalf, and to a speedy public trial by an impartial jury of the county or district in which the offense is alleged to have been committed.

Section 8. Right to Bail – Habeas Corpus

All persons shall be bailable by sufficient sureties, except for capital offenses when proof is evident or presumption great. The privilege of the writ of habeas corpus shall not be suspended unless, when in case of rebellion or invasion, the public safety may require it.

Section 9. Self-Incrimination – Double Jeopardy

No person shall be compelled in any criminal case to give evidence against oneself or be twice put in jeopardy for the same offense.

Section 10. Indictment or Information – Modification or Abolishment of Grand Jury

No person shall be held for a criminal offense unless on the presentment or indictment of a grand jury, or information of the public prosecutor, except in cases of impeachment, in cases cognizable by county courts, by justices of the peace, and in cases arising in the army and navy, or in the militia when in actual service in time of war or public danger: provided, that the grand jury may be modified or abolished by law.

Section 11. Search and Seizure

The right of the people to be secure in their persons, houses, papers and effects, against unreasonable searches and seizures shall not be violated, and no warrant shall issue but upon probable cause supported by affidavit, particularly describing the place to be searched and the person or thing to be seized.

Section 12. Ex Post Facto Laws – Impairment of Contract Obligations – Privilege or Immunity

No ex post facto law, or law impairing the obligation of contracts or making any irrevocable grant of privilege, franchise or immunity, shall be passed.

Section 13. Private Property not Taken Without Just Compensation – Benefit to Owner – Fee in Highways

Private property shall not be taken for public use, or damaged, without just compensation, which will be determined according to legal procedure established by the Legislature and according to Section 6 of this article. No benefit which may accrue to the owner as the result of an improvement made by any private corporation shall be considered in fixing the compensation for property taken or damaged. The fee of land taken for railroad tracks or other highways shall remain in such owners, subject to the use for which it is taken.

Section 14. Resident Alien's Property Rights

No distinction shall ever be made by law between resident aliens and citizens, in reference to the possession, enjoyment or descent of property.

Section 15. Imprisonment for Debt

No person shall be imprisoned for debt arising out of or founded upon a contract.

Section 16. Military Subordinate to Civil Power – Quartering of Soldiers

The military shall be in strict subordination to the civil power. No soldier in time of peace shall be quartered in any house without consent of the owner, nor in time of war except in the manner prescribed by law.

Section 17. Taxation Without Consent – Uniformity

No tax or duty shall be imposed without the consent of the people or their representatives in the Legislature, and all taxation shall be equal and uniform.

Section 18. Equal Privileges or Immunities

No law shall be passed granting to any citizen, class of citizens or corporation, privileges or immunities which upon the same terms shall not equally belong to all citizens or corporations.

Section 19. Free and Equal Elections – Right of Suffrage – Soldier Voting

Elections shall be free and equal, and no power, civil or military, shall at any time interfere to prevent the free exercise of the right of suffrage. Soldiers in time of war may vote at their post of duty in or out of the state, under regulations to be prescribed by the Legislature.

Section 20. Courts Open – Remedy for Injury

All courts shall be open, and every man for an injury done him in his property, person or reputation, shall have remedy by due course of law, and right and justice, administered without denial or delay.

Section 21. Suspension of Laws Prohibited

No power of suspending laws shall be exercised, unless by the Legislature or its authority.

Section 22. Attainder by Legislature Prohibited

No person shall be attainted of treason or felony by the Legislature.

Section 23. Excessive Bail or Fines – Cruel Punishments

Excessive bail shall not be required, excessive fines imposed, nor cruel punishments inflicted.

Section 24. Right to Bear Arms

The right of the citizens to bear arms in defense of themselves and the state shall not be denied.

Section 25. Treason

Treason against the state shall consist only in levying war against it, or in adhering to its enemies or in giving them aid and comfort. No person shall be convicted of treason unless on the testimony of two witnesses to the same overt act or confession in open court.

Section 26. Power Inherent in People – Alteration in Form of Government – Inseparable Part of Union

All political power is inherent in the people, and all free government is founded on their authority, and is instituted for their equal protection and benefit, and they have the right in lawful and constituted methods to alter or reform their forms of government in such manner as they may think proper. And the state of South Dakota is an inseparable part of the American Union and the Constitution of the United States is the supreme law of the land.

Section 27. Maintenance of free government – Fundamental principles. The blessings of a free government can only be maintained by a firm adherence to justice, moderation, temperance, frugality and virtue and by frequent recurrence to fundamental principles.

Section 28. Right to vote by secret ballot

The rights of individuals to vote by secret ballot are fundamental. If any state or federal law requires or permits an election for public office, for any initiative or referendum, or for any designation or authorization of employee representation, the right of any individual to vote by secret ballot shall be guaranteed.

Section 29. Rights of Crime Victim

A victim shall have the following rights, beginning at the time of victimization:

1. The right to due process and to be treated with fairness and respect for the victim's dignity;

2. The right to be free from intimidation, harassment and abuse;

3. The right to be reasonably protected from the accused and any person acting on behalf of the accused;

4. The right to have the safety and welfare of the victim and the victim's family considered when setting bail or making release decisions;

5. The right to prevent the disclosure of information or records that could be used to locate or harass the victim or the victim's family, or which could disclose confidential or privileged information about the victim, and to be notified of any request for such information or records;

6. The right to privacy, which includes the right to refuse an interview, deposition or other discovery request, and to set reasonable conditions on the conduct of any such interaction to which the victim consents;

7. The right to reasonable, accurate and timely notice of, and to be present at, all proceedings involving the criminal or delinquent conduct, including release, plea, sentencing, adjudication and disposition, and any proceeding during which a right of the victim is implicated;

8. The right to be promptly notified of any release or escape of the accused;

9. The right to be heard in any proceeding involving release, plea, sentencing, adjudication, disposition or parole, and any proceeding during which a right of the victim is implicated;

10. The right to confer with the attorney for the government;

11. The right to provide information regarding the impact of the offender's conduct on the victim and the victim's family to the individual responsible for conducting any pre-sentence or disposition sentence investigation report or plan of disposition, and to have any such information considered in any sentencing or disposition recommendations;

12. The right to receive a copy of any pre-sentence report or plan of disposition, and any other report or record relevant to the exercise of a victim's right, except for those portions made confidential by law;

13. The right to the prompt return of the victim's property when no longer needed as evidence in the case;

14. The right to full and timely restitution in every case and from each offender for all losses suffered by the victim as a result of the criminal conduct and as provided by law for all losses suffered as a result of delinquent conduct. All monies and property collected from any person who has been ordered to make restitution shall be first applied to the restitution owed to the victim before paying any amounts owed to the government;

15. The right to proceedings free from unreasonable delay, and to a prompt and final conclusion of the case and any related post-judgment proceedings;

16. The right to be informed of the conviction, adjudication, sentence, disposition, place and time of incarceration, detention or other disposition of the offender, any scheduled release date of the offender, and the release of or the escape by the offender from custody;

17. The right to be informed in a timely manner of all post-judgment processes and procedures, to participate in such processes and procedures, to provide information to the release authority to be considered before any release decision is made, and to be notified of any release decision regarding the offender. Any parole authority shall extend the right to be heard to any person harmed by the offender;

18. The right to be informed in a timely manner of clemency and expungement procedures, to provide information to the Governor, the court, any clemency board and other authority in these procedures, and to have that information considered before a clemency or expungement decision is made, and to be notified of such decision in advance of any release of the offender; and

19. The right to be informed of these rights, and to be informed that a victim can seek the advice of an attorney with respect to the victim's rights. This information shall be made available to the general public and provided to each crime victim in what is referred to as a Marsy's Card.

The victim, the retained attorney of the victim, a lawful representative of the victim, or the attorney for the government, upon request of the victim, may assert and seek enforcement of the rights enumerated in this section and any other right afforded to a victim by law in any trial or appellate court, or before any other authority with jurisdiction over the case, as a matter of right. The court or other authority with jurisdiction shall act promptly on such a request, affording a remedy by due course of law for the violation of any right and ensuring that victims' rights and interests are protected in a manner no less vigorous than the protections afforded to criminal defendants and children accused of delinquency. The reasons for any decision regarding the disposition of a victim's right shall be clearly stated on the record. The granting of these rights to any victim shall ensure the victim has a meaningful role throughout the criminal and juvenile justice systems and may not be construed to deny or disparage other rights possessed by victims. All provisions of this section apply throughout criminal and juvenile justice processes, are self-enabling and require no further action by the Legislature. As used in this section, the term, victim, means a person who suffers direct or threatened physical, psychological, or financial harm as a result of the commission or attempted commission of a crime or delinquent act or against whom the crime or delinquent act is committed. The term also includes any spouse, parent, grandparent, child, sibling, grandchild, or guardian, and any person with a relationship to the victim that is substantially similar to a listed relationship, and includes a lawful representative of a victim who is deceased, incompetent, a minor, or physically or mentally incapacitated. The term does not include the accused or a person whom the court finds would not act in the best interests of a deceased, incompetent, minor or incapacitated victim.

ARTICLE VII: ELECTIONS AND RIGHT OF SUFFRAGE

Section 1. Right to Vote

Elections shall be free and equal, and no power, civil or military, shall at any time interfere to prevent the free exercise of the right of suffrage.

Section 2. Voter Qualification

Every United States citizen eighteen years of age or older who has met all residency and registration requirements shall be entitled to vote in all elections and upon all questions submitted to the voters of the state unless disqualified by law for mental incompetence or the conviction of a felony. The Legislature may by law establish reasonable requirements to insure the integrity of the vote. Each elector who qualified to vote within a precinct shall be entitled to vote in that precinct until he establishes another voting residence. An elector shall never lose his residency for voting solely by reason of his absence from the state.

Section 3. Elections

The Legislature shall by law define residence for voting purposes, insure secrecy in voting and provide for the registration of voters, absentee voting, the administration of elections, the nomination of candidates and the voting rights of those serving in the armed forces. Section

Section 4 to 10.

Superseded

ARTICLE VIII: EDUCATION AND SCHOOL LANDS

Section 1. Uniform System of Free Public Schools

The stability of a republican form of government depending on the morality and intelligence of the people, it shall be the duty of the Legislature to establish and maintain a general and uniform system of public schools wherein tuition shall be without charge, and equally open to all; and to adopt all suitable means to secure to the people the advantages and opportunities of education.

Section 2. Perpetual Trust Fund for Maintenance of Public Schools – Principal Inviolate

All proceeds of the sale of public lands that have heretofore been or may hereafter be given by the United States for the use of public schools in the state; all such per centum as may be granted by the United States on the sales of public lands; the proceeds of all property that shall fall to the state by escheat; the proceeds of all gifts or donations to the state for public schools or not otherwise appropriated by the terms of the gift; and all property otherwise acquired for public schools, shall be and remain a perpetual fund for the maintenance of public schools in the state. It shall be deemed a trust fund held by the state. The principal shall never be diverted by legislative enactment for any other purpose, and may be increased; but, if any loss occurs through any unconstitutional act, the state shall make the loss good through a special appropriation.

Section 3. Fund Income Apportioned Among Schools – Apportionment of Fines

The interest and income of this fund together with all other sums which may be added thereto by law, shall be faithfully used and applied each year for the benefit of the public schools of the state, and shall be for this purpose apportioned among and between all the several public school corporations of the state in proportion to the number of children in each, of school age, as may be fixed by law; and no part of the fund, either principal or interest, shall ever be diverted, by legislative enactment, even temporarily, from this purpose or used for any other purpose whatever than the maintenance of public schools for the equal benefit of all the people of the state. However, before the interest and income is apportioned to the public schools, the principal shall be increased each year by an amount equal to the rate of inflation from the interest and income earned from this fund. The principal may be prudently invested as provided by law. The proceeds of all fines collected from violations of state laws shall be paid to the county treasurer of the county in which the fine was imposed, and distributed by the county treasurer among and between all of the several public schools incorporated in such county in proportion to the number of children in each, of school age, as may be fixed by law.

Section 4. Sale of School Lands – Appraisal

After one year from the assembling of the first Legislature, the lands granted to the state by the United States for the use of public schools may be sold upon the following conditions and no other: not more than one-third of all such lands shall be sold within the first five years, and no more than two-thirds within the first fifteen years after the title thereto is vested in the state, and the Legislature shall, subject to the provisions of this article, provide for the sale of the same. The commissioner of school and public lands, the state auditor and the county superintendent of schools of the counties severally, shall constitute boards of appraisal and shall appraise all school lands within the several counties which they may from time to time select and designate for sale, at their actual value under the terms of sale. They shall take care to first select and designate for sale the most valuable lands; and they shall ascertain all such lands as may be of special and peculiar value, other than agricultural, and cause the proper subdivision of the same in order that the largest price may be obtained therefor.

Section 5. Terms of Sale of School Lands

No land shall be sold for less than the appraised value, and in no case for less than ten dollars per acre. The purchaser shall pay at least one-tenth of the purchase price in cash. The Legislature shall provide by general law for payment of the balance which shall be made in partial payments and must be fully paid up within thirty years. Interest shall be established by the Legislature. All lands may be sold for cash, provided further, that the purchaser or purchasers shall have the right or option of paying the balance in whole or in part on any interest paying date, under such rules as the Legislature may provide. No land shall be sold until appraised and advertised and offered for sale at public auction. No land can be sold except at public sale. Such lands as shall not have been specially subdivided shall be offered in tracts of not more than eighty acres and these subdivided into the smallest division of the lands designated for sale and not sold within two years after their appraisal shall be reappraised by the board of appraisers as hereinafter provided before they are sold.

Section 6. Conduct of Sales of School Lands – Conveyance of Right or Title

All sales shall be conducted through the office of the commissioner of school and public lands as may be prescribed by law, and returns of all appraisals and sales shall be made to said office. No sale shall operate to convey any right or title to any lands for sixty days after the date thereof, nor until the same shall have received the approval of the Governor in such form as may be provided by law. No grant or patent for any such lands shall issue until final payment be made.

Section 7. Perpetual Trust Fund From Proceeds of Grants and Gifts

All lands, money, or other property donated, granted, or received from the United States or any other source for a university, agricultural college, normal schools , or other educational or charitable institution or purpose, and the proceeds of all such lands and other property so received from any source, shall be and remain perpetual funds, the interest and income of which, together with the rents of all such lands as may remain unsold, shall be inviolably appropriated and applied to the specific objects of the original grants or gifts. The principal of every such fund may be increased, but shall never be diverted by legislative enactment for any other purpose, and the interest and income only shall be used. Every such fund shall be deemed a trust fund held by the state, and the state shall make good all losses that may occur through any unconstitutional act or where required under the Enabling Act.

Section 8. Appraisal and Sale of Donated Lands – Separate Accounts

All lands mentioned in the preceding section shall be appraised and sold in the same manner and by the same officers and boards under the same limitations, and subject to all the conditions as to price, sale and approval, provided above for the appraisal and sale of lands for the benefit of public schools, but a distinct and separate account shall be kept by the proper officers of each of such funds.

Section 9. Lease of School Lands

The lands mentioned in this article shall be leased for pasturage, meadow, farming, the growing of crops of grain and general agricultural purposes, and at public auction after notice as hereinbefore provided in case of sale and shall be offered in tracts not greater than one section. All rents shall be payable annually in advance, and no term of lease shall exceed five years, nor shall any lease be valid until it receives the approval of the Governor. Provided, that any lessee of school and public lands shall, at the expiration of a five-year lease, be entitled, at his option, to a new lease for the land included in his original lease, for a period of time not exceeding five years, without public advertising, at the current rental prevailing in the county in which such land is situated, at the time of the issuance of the new lease. The commissioner of school and public lands shall notify by registered mail each lessee or assignee on or before the first day of November first preceding the expiration of his lease that such lease will expire. Such option shall be exercised by the lessee by notifying the commissioner of school and public lands by registered mail, on or before the first day of December first preceding the expiration of his lease describing the lands for which he desires a new lease, in the same manner as the same is described in his original lease. The Legislature may provide by appropriate legislation for the payment of local property taxes by the lessees of school and public lands.

Section 10. Trespassers Claims to Public Lands not Recognized – Improvements not Compensated

No claim to any public lands by any trespasser thereon by reason of occupancy, cultivation or improvement thereof, shall ever be recognized; nor shall compensation ever be made on account of any improvements made by such trespasser.

Section 11. Investment of Permanent Educational Funds

Except as otherwise required by the Enabling Act, the moneys of the permanent school and other educational and charitable funds shall be invested by the state investment council in stocks, bonds, mutual funds, and other financial instruments as provided by law.

Section 12. Disapproval by Governor of Sale, Lease or Investment

The Governor may disapprove any sale, lease or investment other than such as are in trusted to the counties.

Section 13. Audit of Losses to Permanent Educational Funds – Permanent Debt – Interest

The permanent school or other educational and charitable funds of this state shall be audited by the proper authorities of the state. If any loss occurs through any unconstitutional act, the state shall make the loss good through a special appropriation. The amount of indebtedness so created shall not be counted as a part of the indebtedness mentioned in article XIII, Section 2.

Section 14. Protection and Defense of School Lands

The Legislature shall provide by law for the protection of the school lands from trespass or unlawful appropriation, and for their defense against all unauthorized claims or efforts to divert them from the school fund.

Section 15. Taxation to Support School System – Classification of Property

The Legislature shall make such provision by general taxation and by authorizing the school corporations to levy such additional taxes as with the income from the permanent school fund shall secure a thorough and efficient system of common schools throughout the state. The Legislature is empowered to classify properties within school districts into separate classes for purposes of school taxation. Taxes shall be uniform on all property in the same class.

Section 16. Public Support of Sectarian Instruction Prohibited

No appropriation of lands, money or other property or credits to aid any sectarian school shall ever be made by the state, or any county or municipality within the state, nor shall the state or any county or municipality within the state accept any grant, conveyance, gift or bequest of lands, money or other property to be used for sectarian purposes, and no sectarian instruction shall be allowed in any school or institution aided or supported by the state.

Section 17. Interest in Sale of School Equipment Prohibited

No teacher, state, county, township or district school officer shall be interested in the sale, proceeds or profits of any book, apparatus or furniture used or to be used in any school in this state, under such penalties as shall be provided by law.

Section 18. Apportionment of Mineral Leasing Moneys – Amounts Covered into Permanent Funds

Notwithstanding the provisions of Section Section 2, 3 and 7 of article VIII of this Constitution, moneys received from the leasing of all common school, indemnity, and endowment lands for oil and gas and other mineral leasing of said lands shall be apportioned among the public schools and the various state institutions in such manner that the public schools and each of such institutions shall receive an amount which bears the same ratio to the total amount apportioned as the number of acres (including any that may have been disposed of) granted for such public schools or for such institutions bears to the total number of acres (including any that may have been disposed of) granted in trust to the state by the Enabling Act approved February 22, 1889, as amended, and allocations authorized pursuant to the provisions of Section 17 of such Enabling Act; and further that not less than fifty percent of each such amount so allocated shall be covered into the permanent fund of the public schools and each of such institutions.

Section 19. Mineral Rights Reserved to State – Leases Permitted

All gas, coal, oil and mineral rights, and any other rights, as specified by law, to or in public lands, are reserved for the state. Leases may be executed by the state for the exploration, extraction and sale of such materials in the manner and with such conditions as are provided by law.

Section 20. Loan of Nonsectarian Textbooks to all School Children

Notwithstanding the provisions of section 3, Article VI and section 16, Article VIII, the Legislature may authorize the loaning of nonsectarian textbooks to all children of school age.

ARTICLE IX: LOCAL GOVERNMENT

Section 1. Organization of Local Government

The Legislature shall have plenary powers to organize and classify units of local government, except that any proposed change in county boundaries shall be submitted to the voters of each affected county at an election and be approved by a majority of those voting thereon in each county. No township heretofore organized may be abolished unless the question is submitted to the voters of the township and approved by a majority of those voting thereon in each township.

Section 2. Home Rule

Any county or city or combinations thereof may provide for the adoption or amendment of a charter. Such charter shall be adopted or amended if approved at an election by a majority of the votes cast thereon. Not less than ten percent of those voting in the last preceding gubernatorial election in the affected jurisdiction may by petition initiate the question of whether to adopt or amend a charter. A chartered governmental unit may exercise any legislative power or perform any function not denied by its charter, the Constitution or the general laws of the state. The charter may provide for any form of executive, legislative and administrative structure which shall be of superior authority to statute, provided that the legislative body so established be chosen by popular election and that the administrative proceedings be subject to judicial review. Powers and functions of home rule units shall be construed liberally.

Section 3. Intergovernmental Cooperation

Every local government may exercise, perform or transfer any of its powers or functions, including financing the same, jointly or in cooperation with any other governmental entities, either within or without the state, except as the Legislature shall provide otherwise by law.

Section 4. Local Initiatives to Provide for Cooperation and Organization of Local Government Units

On or after January 1, 2001, the voters of any unit of local government shall have the right to initiate proposals for cooperation within or between local governmental units, either within or without the state, except as the Legislature shall provide otherwise by law. Such proposals may include combining, eliminating, and joint financing of offices, functions, and governmental units. Such proposals shall be adopted if approved at an election by a majority of the votes cast thereon in each affected unit. A number not less than fifteen percent of those voting in the last preceding gubernatorial election in each affected jurisdiction may by petition initiate the question of whether to adopt the proposal at the next general election.

Section Section 5 to 7.

Superseded

ARTICLE X: MUNICIPAL CORPORATIONS

Repealed

ARTICLE XI: REVENUE AND FINANCE

Section 1. Annual Tax

The Legislature shall provide for an annual tax, sufficient to defray the estimated ordinary expenses of the state for each year, not to exceed in any one year two mills on each dollar of the assessed valuation of all taxable property in the state, to be ascertained by the last assessment made for state and county purposes. And whenever it shall appear that such ordinary expenses shall exceed the income of the state for such year, the Legislature shall provide for levying a tax for the ensuing year, sufficient, with other sources of income, to pay the deficiency of the preceding year, together with the estimated expenses of such ensuing year. And for the purpose of paying the public debt, the Legislature shall provide for levying a tax annually, sufficient to pay the annual interest and the principal of such debt within ten years from the final passage of the law creating the debt; provided, that the annual tax for the payment of the interest and principal of the public debt shall not exceed in any one year two mills on each dollar of the assessed valuation of all taxable property in the state, as ascertained by the last assessment made for the state and county purposes. Provided, that for the purpose of establishing, installing, maintaining and operating a hard fiber twine and cordage plant at the state penitentiary at Sioux Falls, South Dakota, the Legislature shall provide for a tax for the year 1907 of not to exceed one and one-half mills on each dollar of the assessed valuation of all taxable property in the state, as ascertained by the last assessment made for state and county purposes.

Section 2. Classification of Property for Taxation – Income

To the end that the burden of taxation may be equitable upon all property, and in order that no property which is made subject to taxation shall escape, the Legislature is empowered to divide all property including moneys and credits as well as physical property into classes and to determine what class or classes of property shall be subject to taxation and what property, if any, shall not be subject to taxation. Taxes shall be uniform on all property of the same class, and shall be levied and collected for public purposes only. Taxes may be imposed upon any and all property including privileges, franchises and licenses to do business in the state. Gross earnings and net incomes may be considered in taxing any and all property, and the valuation of property for taxation purposes shall never exceed the actual value thereof. The Legislature is empowered to impose taxes upon incomes and occupations, and taxes upon incomes may be graduated and progressive and reasonable exemptions may be provided.

Section 3. Corporate Tax Power of State not Suspended

The power to tax corporations and corporate property shall not be surrendered or suspended by any contract or grant to which the state shall be a party.

Section 4. Banks and Bankers Taxed

The Legislature shall provide for taxing all moneys, credits, investments in bonds, stocks, joint stock companies, or otherwise; and also for taxing the notes and bills discounted or purchased, moneys loaned and all other property, effects or dues of every description, of all banks and of all bankers, so that all property employed in banking shall always be subject to a taxation equal to that imposed on the property of individuals.

Section 5. Public Property Exempt from Taxation – Exceptions

The property of the United States and of the state, county and municipal corporations, both real and personal, shall be exempt from taxation, provided, however, that all state owned lands acquired under the provisions of the rural credit act may be taxed by the local taxing districts for county, township and school purposes, and all state owned lands, known as public shooting areas, acquired under the provisions of Section 25.0106 SDC

1939 and acts amendatory thereto, may be taxed by the local taxing districts for county, township and school purposes in such manner as the Legislature may provide.

Section 6. Property Exempt from Taxation – Personal Property

The Legislature shall, by general law, exempt from taxation, property used exclusively for agricultural and horticultural societies, for school, religious, cemetery and charitable purposes, property acquired and used exclusively for public highway purposes, and personal property to any amount not exceeding in value two hundred dollars for each individual liable to taxation.

Section 7. Other Exemption Laws Void

All laws exempting property from taxation other than that enumerated in Section Section 5 and 6 of this article, shall be void.

Section 8. Object of Tax to be Stated – Use of Vehicle and Fuel Taxes

No tax shall be levied except in pursuance of a law, which shall distinctly state the object of the same, to which the tax only shall be applied, and the proceeds from the imposition of any license, registration fee, or other charge with respect to the operation of any motor vehicle upon any public highways in this state and the proceeds from the imposition of any excise tax on gasoline or other liquid motor fuel except costs of administration and except the tax imposed upon gasoline or other liquid motor fuel not used to propel a motor vehicle over or upon public highways of this state shall be used exclusively for the maintenance, construction and supervision of highways and bridges of this state.

Section 9. Taxes Paid into Treasury – Appropriations Required for Expenditure

All taxes levied and collected for state purposes shall be paid into the state treasury. No indebtedness shall be incurred or money expended by the state, and no warrant shall be drawn upon the state treasurer except in pursuance of an appropriation for the specific purpose first made. The Legislature shall provide by suitable enactment for carrying this section into effect.

Section 10. Special Assessments for Local Improvements – Taxes for Municipal Purposes

The Legislature may vest the corporate authority of cities, towns and villages, with power to make local improvements by special taxation of contiguous property or otherwise. For all corporate purposes, all municipal corporations may be vested with authority to assess and collect taxes; but such tax shall be uniform in respect to persons and property within the jurisdiction of the body levying the same.

Section 11. Unauthorized use of Public Money as Felony

The making of profit, directly or indirectly, out of state, county, city, town or school district money, or using the same for any purpose not authorized by law, shall be deemed a felony and shall be punished as provided by law.

Section 12. Annual Statement of Receipts and Expenditures

An accurate statement of the receipts and expenditures of the public moneys shall be published annually, in such manner as the Legislature may provide.

Section 13. Vote Required to Increase Tax Rates or Valuations

The rate of taxation imposed by the state of South Dakota on personal or corporate income or on sales or services, or the allowable levies or the percentage basis for determining valuation as fixed by law for purposes of taxation on real or personal property, shall not be increased unless by consent of the people by exercise of their right of initiative or by two-thirds vote of all the members elect of each branch of the Legislature.

Section 14. Vote Required to Impose or Increase Taxes

The rate of taxation imposed by the State of South Dakota in regard to any tax may not be increased and no new tax may be imposed by the State of South Dakota unless by consent of the people by exercise of their right of initiative or by two-thirds vote of all the members elect of each branch of the Legislature.

Section 15. Inheritance Tax Prohibited

No tax may be levied on any inheritance, and the Legislature may not enact any law imposing such a tax. The effective date of this section is July 1, 2001.

ARTICLE XII: PUBLIC ACCOUNTS AND EXPENDITURES

Section 1. Appropriation and Warrant Required for Payment from Treasury

No money shall be paid out of the treasury except upon appropriation by law and on warrant drawn by the proper officer.

Section 2. Contents of General Appropriation Bill – Separate Appropriation Bills

The general appropriation bill shall embrace nothing but appropriations for ordinary expenses of the executive, legislative and judicial departments of the state, the current expenses of state institutions, interest on the public debt, and for common schools. All other appropriations shall be made by separate bills, each embracing but one object, and shall require a two-thirds vote of all the members of each branch of the Legislature.

Section 3. Extra Compensation Prohibited – Unauthorized Contracts – Change in Compensation of Officers – Appropriations for Defense of State

The Legislature shall never grant any extra compensation to any public officer, employee, agent or contractor after the services shall have been rendered or the contract entered into, nor authorize the payment of any claims or part thereof created against the state, under any agreement or contract made without express authority of law, and all such unauthorized agreements or contracts shall be null and void; nor shall the compensation of any public officer be increased or diminished during his term of office: provided, however, that the Legislature may make appropriations for expenditures incurred in suppressing insurrection or repelling invasion.

Section 4. Annual Statement Required

An itemized statement of all receipts and expenditures of the public moneys shall be published annually in such manner as the Legislature shall provide, and such statement shall be submitted to the Legislature at the beginning of each regular session by the Governor with his message.

Section 5. Health Care Trust Fund Established - Investment – Appropriations

There is hereby created in the state treasury a trust fund named the health care trust fund. The state treasurer shall deposit into the health care trust fund any funds on deposit in the intergovernmental transfer fund as of July 1, 2001, and thereafter any funds appropriated to the health care trust fund as provided by law. The South Dakota Investment Council or its successor shall invest the health care trust fund in stocks, bonds, mutual funds, and other financial instruments as provided by law. Beginning in fiscal year 2003, and each year thereafter, the state treasurer shall make a distribution from the health care trust fund into the state general fund to be appropriated by law for health care related programs. The calculation of the distribution shall be defined by law and may promote growth of the fund and a steadily growing distribution amount. The health care trust fund may not be diverted for other purposes nor may the principal be invaded unless appropriated by a three-fourths vote of all the members-elect of each house of the Legislature.

Section 6. Education Enhancement Trust Fund Established - Investment – Appropriations

There is hereby created in the state treasury a trust fund named the education enhancement trust fund. The state treasurer shall deposit into the education enhancement trust fund any funds received as of July 1, 2001, and funds received thereafter by the state pursuant to the Master Settlement Agreement entered into on November 23, 1998, by the State of South Dakota and major

United States tobacco product manufacturers or the net proceeds of any sale or securitization of rights to receive payments pursuant to the Master Settlement Agreement, any funds in the youth-at- risk trust fund as of July 1, 2001, and thereafter any funds appropriated to the education enhancement trust fund as provided by law. The South Dakota Investment Council or its successor shall invest the education enhancement trust fund in stocks, bonds, mutual funds, and other financial instruments as provided by law. Beginning in fiscal year 2003, and each year thereafter, the state treasurer shall make a distribution from the education enhancement trust fund into the state general fund to be appropriated by law for education enhancement programs. The calculation of the distribution shall be defined by law and may promote growth of the fund and a steadily growing distribution amount. The education enhancement trust fund may not be diverted for other purposes nor may the principal be invaded unless appropriated by a three-fourths vote of all the members-elect of each house of the Legislature.

ARTICLE XIII: PUBLIC INDEBTEDNESS

Section 1. State Enterprises – Legislative Vote Required – Defense of State – Rural Credits – Maximum Indebtedness

For the purpose of developing the resources and improving the economic facilities of South Dakota, the state may engage in works of internal improvement, may own and conduct proper business enterprises, may loan or give its credit to, or in aid of, any association, or corporation, organized for such purposes. But any such association or corporation shall be subject to regulation and control by the state as may be provided by law. No money of the state shall be appropriated, or indebtedness incurred for any of the purposes of this section, except by the vote of two-thirds of the members of each branch of the Legislature. The state may also assume or pay any debt or liability incurred in time of war for the defense of the state. The state may establish and maintain a system of rural credits and thereby loan and extend credit to the people of the state upon real estate security in such manner and upon such terms and conditions as may be prescribed by general law. The limit of indebtedness contained in Section 2 of this article shall not apply to the provisions of this section, but the indebtedness of the state for the purposes contained in this section shall never exceed one-half of one percent of the assessed valuation of the property of the state, provided however, that nothing contained in this section shall affect the refinancing or refunding of the present outstanding indebtedness of this state.

Section 2. Maximum State Debt – Irrepealable Tax to Repay

For the purpose of defraying extraordinary expenses and making public improvements, or to meet casual deficits or failure in revenue, the state may contract debts never to exceed with previous debts in the aggregate one hundred thousand dollars, and no greater indebtedness shall be incurred except for the purpose of repelling invasion, suppressing insurrection, or defending thee state or the United States in war and provision shall be made by law for the payment of the interest annually, and the principal when due, by tax levied for the purpose or from other sources of revenue; which law providing for the payment of such interest and principal by such tax or otherwise shall be irrepealable until such debt is paid: provided, however, the state of South Dakota shall have the power to refund the territorial debt assumed by the state of South Dakota, by bonds of the state of South Dakota.

Section 3. State Debt as in Addition to Territorial Debt

That the indebtedness of the state of South Dakota limited by Section 2 of this article shall be in addition to the debt of the territory of Dakota assumed by and agreed to be paid by South Dakota.

45
Section 4. Debt Limitations for Municipalities and Political Subdivisions

The debt of any county, city, town or civil township shall never exceed five per centum upon the assessed valuation of the taxable property therein, for the year preceding that in which said indebtedness is incurred. The debt of any school district shall never exceed ten per centum upon the assessed valuation of the taxable property therein, for the year preceding that in which said indebtedness is incurred. In estimating the amount of the indebtedness which a municipality or subdivision may incur, the amount of indebtedness contracted prior to the adoption of the Constitution shall be included. Provided, that any county, municipal corporation, civil township, district, or other subdivision may incur an additional indebtedness, not exceeding ten per centum upon the assessed valuation of the taxable property therein, for the year preceding that in which said indebtedness is incurred, for the purpose of providing water and sewerage, for irrigation, domestic uses, sewerage and other purposes; and Provided, further, that in a city where the population is eight thousand or more, such city may incur an indebtedness not exceeding eight per centum upon the assessed valuation of the taxable property therein for the year next preceding that in which said indebtedness is incurred for the purpose of constructing street railways, electric lights or other lighting plants. Provided, further, that no county, municipal corporation, civil township, district or subdivision shall be included within such district or subdivision without a majority vote in favor thereof of the electors of the county, municipal corporation, civil township, district or other subdivision, as the case may be, which is proposed to be included therein, and no such debt shall ever be incurred for any of the purposes in this section provided, unless authorized by a vote in favor thereof by a majority of the electors of such county, municipal corporation, civil township, district or subdivision incurring the same.

Section 5. Irrepealable Tax to Repay Debt of Municipality or Political Subdivision

Any city, county, town, school district or any other subdivision incurring indebtedness shall, at or before the time of so doing, provide for the collection of an annual tax sufficient to pay the interest and also the principal thereof when due, and all laws or ordinances providing for the payment of the interest or principal of any debt shall be irrepealable until such debt be paid.

Section 6. Adjustment of Debts and Liabilities of Territory Of Dakota

In order that payment of the debts and liabilities contracted or incurred by and in behalf of the territory of Dakota may be justly and equitably provided for and made, and in pursuance of the requirements of an act of Congress approved February 22, 1889, entitled "An act to provide for the division of Dakota into two states and to enable the people of North Dakota, South Dakota, Montana and Washington to form Constitutions and state governments and to be admitted into the union on an equal footing with the original states, and to make donations of public lands to such states" the states of North Dakota and South

Dakota, by proceedings of a joint commission, duly appointed under said act, the sessions whereof were held at Bismarck in said state of North Dakota, from July 16, 1889, to July 31, 1889, inclusive, have agreed to the following adjustment of the amounts of the debts and liabilities of the territory of Dakota which shall be assumed and paid by each of the states of North Dakota and South Dakota, respectively, to wit:

1. This agreement shall take effect and be in force from and after the admission into the union, as one of the United States of America, of either the state of North Dakota or the state of South Dakota.

2. The words "state of North Dakota" wherever used in this agreement, shall be taken to mean the territory of North Dakota, in case the state of South Dakota shall be admitted into the union prior to the admission into the union of the state of North Dakota; and the words "state of South Dakota," wherever used in this agreement, shall be taken to mean the territory of South Dakota in case the state of North Dakota shall be admitted into the union prior to the admission into the union of the state of South Dakota.

3. The said state of North Dakota shall assume and pay all bonds issued by the territory of Dakota to provide funds for the purchase, construction, repairs or maintenance of such public institutions, grounds or buildings as are located within the boundaries of North Dakota, and shall pay all warrants issued under and by virtue of that certain act of the legislative assembly of the territory of Dakota, approved March 3, 1889, entitled an act to provide for the refunding of outstanding warrants drawn on the capitol building fund.

4. The said state of South Dakota shall assume and pay all bonds issued by the territory of Dakota to provide funds for the purchase, construction, repairs or maintenance of such public institutions, grounds or buildings as are located within the boundaries of South Dakota.

5. That is to say: The state of North Dakota shall assume and pay the following bonds and indebtedness, to wit: Bonds issued on account of the hospital for insane at Jamestown, North Dakota, the face aggregate of which is two hundred and sixty-six thousand dollars; also, bonds issued on account of the North Dakota University at Grand Forks, North Dakota, the face aggregate of which is ninety-six thousand seven hundred dollars; also, bonds issued on account of the penitentiary at Bismarck, North Dakota, the face aggregate of which is ninety-three thousand six hundred dollars; also, refunding capitol building warrants dated April 1, 1889, eighty-three thousand five hundred and seven dollars and forty-six cents. And the state of South Dakota shall assume and pay the following bonds and indebtedness, to wit: Bonds issued on account of the hospital for the insane at Yankton, South Dakota, the face aggregate of which is two hundred and ten thousand dollars; also, bonds issued on account of the school for deaf mutes, at Sioux Falls, South Dakota, the face aggregate of which is fifty-one thousand dollars; also, bonds issued on account of the university at Vermillion, South Dakota, the face aggregate of which is seventy-five thousand dollars; also, bonds issued on account of the penitentiary at Sioux Falls, South Dakota, the face aggregate of which is ninety-four thousand three hundred dollars; also, bonds issued on account of agricultural college at Brookings, South Dakota, the face aggregate of which is ninety-seven thousand five hundred dollars; also, bonds issued on account of the normal school at Madison, South Dakota, the face aggregate of which is forty-nine thousand four hundred dollars; also, bonds issued on account of school of mines at Rapid City, South Dakota, the face aggregate of which is thirty-three thousand dollars; also, bonds issued on account of the reform school at Plankinton, South Dakota, the face aggregate of which is thirty thousand dollars; also, bonds issued on account of the normal school at Spearfish, South Dakota, the face aggregate of which is twenty-five thousand dollars; also, bonds issued on account of the soldiers' home at Hot Springs, South Dakota, the face aggregate of which is forty-five thousand dollars.

6. The states of North Dakota and South Dakota shall pay one-half each of all liabilities now existing or hereafter and prior to the taking effect of this agreement incurred, except those heretofore and hereafter incurred on account of public institutions, grounds or buildings, except as otherwise herein specifically provided.

7. The state of South Dakota shall pay to the state of North Dakota forty-six thousand five hundred dollars on account of the excess of territorial appropriations for the permanent improvement of territorial institutions which under this agreement will go to South Dakota, and in full of the undivided one-half interest of North Dakota in the territorial library and in full settlement of unbalanced accounts, and of all claims against the territory, of whatever nature, legal or equitable, arising out of the alleged erroneous or unlawful taxation of the Northern Pacific Railroad lands, and the payment of said amount shall discharge and exempt the state of South Dakota from all liability for or on account of the several matters hereinbefore referred to; nor shall either state be called upon to pay or answer to any portion of liability hereafter arising or accruing on account of transactions heretofore had, which liability would be a liability of the territory of Dakota had such territory remained in existence, and which liability shall grow out of matters connected with any public institution, grounds or buildings of the territory situated or located within the boundaries of the other state.

8. A final adjustment of accounts shall be made upon the following basis: North Dakota shall be charged with all sums paid on account of the public institutions, grounds or buildings located within its boundaries on account of the current appropriations since March 8, 1889; and South Dakota shall be charged with all sums paid on account of public institutions, grounds or buildings located within its boundaries on the same account and during the same time. Each state shall be charged with one-half of all other expenses of the territorial government during the same time. All moneys paid into the treasury during the period from March 8, 1889, to the time of taking effect of this agreement by any county, municipality or person within the limits of the proposed state of North Dakota shall be credited to the state of North Dakota; and all sums paid into said treasury within the same time by any county, municipality or person within the limits of the proposed state of South Dakota shall be credited to the state of South Dakota; except that any and all taxes on gross earnings paid into said treasury by railroad corporations since the eighth day of March 1889, based upon earnings of years prior to 1888, under and by virtue of the act of the legislative assembly of the territory of Dakota, approved March 7, 1889, and entitled "An act providing for the levy and collection of taxes upon property of railroad companies in this territory," being chapter 107 of the Session Laws of 1889 (that is, the part of such sum going to the territory) shall be equally divided between the states of North Dakota and South Dakota; and all taxes heretofore or hereafter paid into said treasury under and by virtue of the act last mentioned, based on the gross earnings of the year 1888, shall be distributed as already provided by law, except that so much thereof as goes to the territorial treasury shall be divided as follows: North Dakota shall have so (much) thereof as shall be or has been paid by railroads within the limits of the proposed state of North Dakota and South Dakota so much thereof as shall be or has been paid by railroads within the limits of the proposed state of South Dakota. Each state shall be credited also with all balances of appropriations made by the seventeenth legislative assembly of the territory of Dakota for the account of public institutions, grounds or buildings situated within its limits, remaining unexpended on March 8, 1889. If there be any indebtedness except the indebtedness represented by the bonds and refunding warrants hereinbefore mentioned, each state shall at the time of such final adjustment of accounts, assume its share of said indebtedness as determined by the amount paid on account of the public institutions, grounds or buildings of such state in excess of the receipts from counties, municipalities, railroad corporations or persons within the limits of said state as provided in this article; and if there should be a surplus at the time of such final adjustment, each state shall be entitled to the amounts received from counties, municipalities, railroad corporations or persons within its limits over and above the amount charged to it.

Section 7. Obligation of State to Pay Proportion of Territorial Debt

And the state of South Dakota hereby obligates itself to pay such part of the debts and liabilities of the territory of Dakota as is declared by the foregoing agreement to be its proportion thereof, the same as if such proportion had been originally created by said state of South Dakota as its own debt or liability.

Section 8. Refunding Bond Issue Authorized for Territorial Debt Payment

The territorial treasurer is hereby authorized and empowered to issue refunding bonds to the amount of one hundred seven thousand five hundred dollars, bearing interest not to exceed the rate of four percent per annum, for the purpose of refunding the following described indebtedness of the territory of Dakota, to wit: Seventy-seven thousand five hundred dollars, five percent bonds, dated May 1, 1883, issued for the construction of the west wing of the insane hospital at Yankton and thirty thousand dollars, six percent bonds dated May 1, 1883, issued for permanent improvements [of the] Dakota penitentiary, at Sioux Falls, such refunding bonds, if issued, to run for not more than twenty years, and shall be executed by the Governor and treasurer of the territory, and shall be attested by the secretary under the great seal of the territory. In case such bonds are issued by the territorial treasurer as hereinbefore set forth, before the first day of October, 1889, then upon the admission of South Dakota as a state it shall assume and pay said bonds in lieu of the aforesaid territorial indebtedness.

Section 9. Road Construction and Coal Supply by State

The construction and maintenance of good roads and the supplying of coal to the people of the state from the lands belonging to the state are works of necessity and importance in which the state may engage but no expenditure of money for the same shall be made except by the vote of a two-thirds majority of the Legislature.

Section 10. State Cement Enterprises

The manufacture, distribution and sale of cement and cement products are hereby declared to be works of public necessity and importance in which the state may engage, and suitable laws may be enacted by the Legislature to empower the state to acquire, by purchase or appropriation, all lands, easements, rights of way, tracks, structures, equipment, cars, motive power, implements, facilities, instrumentalities and material, incident or necessary to carry the provisions of this section into effect: provided, however, that no expenditure of money for the purposes enumerated in this section shall be made, except upon a vote of two-thirds of the members elect of each branch of the Legislature.

Section 11. State Pledge to Fund Cement Enterprises

The state may pledge such cement plants and all of the accessories thereto, and may pledge the credit of the state, to provide funds for the purposes enumerated in Section 10 of this article, any provision in this Constitution to the contrary notwithstanding.

Section 12. State Electric Power Enterprises

The manufacture, distribution and sale of electric current for heating, lighting and power purposes are hereby declared to be works of public necessity and importance in which the state may engage, and suitable laws may be enacted by the Legislature to empower the state to acquire, by purchase or appropriation all lands, easements, rights of way, tracks, structures, equipment, cars, motive power, implements, facilities, instrumentalities and material incident or necessary to the acquisition, ownership, control, development and operation of the water powers of this state, and to carry this provision into effect: provided, however, that no expenditure of money for the purposes enumerated in this section shall be made except by a vote of two-thirds of the members elect of each branch of the Legislature.

Section 13. State Pledge to Fund Electric Power Enterprises

The state may pledge such plants and all of the accessories thereto, and may pledge the credit of the state, to provide funds for the purposes enumerated in Section 12 of this article, any provision in this Constitution to the contrary notwithstanding.

Section 14. State Coal Mining Enterprises

The mining, distribution and sale of coal are hereby declared to be works of public necessity and importance in which the state may engage, and the Legislature may enact suitable laws to carry this provision into effect and to empower the state to acquire, by purchase or appropriation, all lands, structures, easements, tracks, rights of way, equipment, cars, motive power, and all other facilities, implements, instrumentalities, and materials necessary or incidental to the acquisition, mining, manufacturing and distribution of coal for fuel purposes: provided, however, that no expenditure of money for the purposes enumerated in this section shall be made except upon a vote of two-thirds of the members elect of each branch of the Legislature.

Section 15. State Pledge to Fund Coal Enterprises

The state may pledge such plants and all of the accessories thereto, as well as the credit of this state, to provide funds for the purposes enumerated in Section 14 of this article, any provision in this Constitution to the contrary notwithstanding.

Section 16. Works of Internal Improvement – State Indebtedness

The state may engage in works of internal improvement, any provision in this Constitution, or limitation in Section 2 of this article, to the contrary notwithstanding. The indebtedness of the state for the purposes contained in this section shall never exceed one-half of one percent of the assessed valuation of all property in this state and no such indebtedness shall be incurred nor money expended, except upon a two-thirds vote of the members elect in each branch of the Legislature.

Section 17. Home Loans by State – Debt Limitation Inapplicable

The state may establish and maintain a system of credits for assisting in the building of homes by the people of the state, and therefor may loan money and extend credit to the people of the state upon real estate security in such manner and upon such terms and conditions as may be prescribed by general law. The limitations and provisions regarding the incurring of indebtedness elsewhere found in the Constitution shall not apply to this section, but the Legislature shall, at the time of incurring any indebtedness hereunder, provide for discharging same.

Section 18. Compensation of Military and War Relief Personnel – Maximum Indebtedness

The Legislature shall be authorized to provide by law for compensating honorably discharged soldiers, sailors, marines, and others, who have served with the armed forces of the United States, or who have engaged in war relief work in the World's War, or other wars of the United States, including former American citizens, who served in allied armies against the central powers in the World's War and who have been honorably discharged and repatriated; such compensation not to exceed the sum of fifteen dollars per month for the period of such service. For this purpose the Legislature may use the credit of the state, and any indebtedness created for this purpose shall not be a part of the indebtedness authorized or limited by other provisions of the Constitution; provided, that the amount of all indebtedness created by the state for the purposes specified in this section shall not exceed six million dollars.

Section 19. Bonus Paid to Veterans and Deceased Veterans Dependents

1. The Legislature shall be authorized to provide by law for compensating and paying a bonus in money to veterans and to dependents of deceased veterans, who were legal residents of the state of South Dakota for a period of not less than six months immediately preceding entry into the armed forces of the United States and who have served for ninety or more days in the armed forces of the United States between the period beginning December 7, 1941 and ending September 2, 1945 and who are still in the armed forces or were discharged therefrom under conditions other than dishonorable. Such bonus to be paid in cash, at the rate of fifty cents per day for each day of service in the armed forces within continental United States and at the rate of seventy-five cents per day for each day of service in the armed forces outside of continental United States, provided that any such person who served wholly within continental United States shall be entitled to receive not to exceed a bonus or total sum of five hundred dollars, and any such person who has served wholly outside of continental United States, or partly within and partly without, shall be entitled to receive not to exceed a bonus payment in the total sum of six hundred fifty dollars; such bonus to be paid on or before the thirty-first day of December 1950. For this purpose the Legislature may use credit of the state and any indebtedness created for this purpose shall not be a part of the indebtedness authorized or limited by other provisions of the Constitution; provided that the amount of indebtedness created by the state for the purpose specified in this section shall not exceed thirty million dollars. If upon computation the amount of thirty million dollars shall be inadequate to make the specified payments as stated in this section, the Legislature shall have the power to apportion the amount.

2. The term "armed forces" shall mean and include the following: United States army, army of the United States, United States navy, United States naval reserves, United States marine corps, United States marine corps reserve, United States coast guard, United States coast guard reserve which shall be construed to include the United States guard temporary reserve, women's army corps, United States navy women's reserve, United States marine corps women's reserve, United States coast guard women's reserve, army nurse corps and navy nurse corps.

Section 20. Trust Fund Created from Proceeds of State Cement Enterprise – Investment

The net proceeds derived from the sale of state cement enterprises shall be deposited by the South Dakota Cement Commission in a trust fund hereby created to benefit the citizens of South Dakota. The South Dakota Investment Council or its successor shall invest the trust fund in stocks, bonds, mutual funds, and other financial instruments as provided by law.

Section 21. Transfers from Trust Fund to General Fund in Support of Education

The Legislature shall transfer from the trust fund to the state general fund four percent of the lesser of the average market value of the trust fund determined by adding the market value of the trust fund at the end of the sixteen most recent calendar quarters as of December thirty-first of that year and dividing that sum by sixteen, or the market value of the trust fund at the end of that calendar year for the support of education in South Dakota. The transfer shall be made prior to June thirtieth of the subsequent calendar year.

ARTICLE XIV: STATE INSTITUTIONS

Section 1. Charitable and Penal Institutions

The charitable and penal institutions of the state of South Dakota shall consist of a penitentiary, a hospital for the mentally ill, a school for the developmentally disabled, and a reform school for juveniles.

Section 2. Government of Charitable and Penal Institutions

The state institutions provided for in the preceding section shall be governed under such rules and restrictions as the Legislature shall provide.

Section 3. Governance of State Educational Institutions

The state university, the agriculture college, the school of mines and technology, the normal schools, a school for the deaf, a school for the blind, and all other educational institutions that may be sustained either wholly or in part by the state and that offer academic or professional degrees of associate of arts, associate of sciences, baccalaureate or greater, shall be under the control of a board of five members appointed by the Governor and confirmed by the senate under such rules and restrictions as the Legislature shall provide. The Legislature may increase the number of members to nine. Postsecondary technical education institutes that offer career and technical associate of applied science degrees and certificates or their successor equivalents and that are funded wholly or in part by the state shall be separately governed as determined by the Legislature.

Section 4. Repealed

Section 5. Mining and Metallurgy to be Taught

The Legislature shall provide that the science of mining and metallurgy be taught in at least one institution of learning under the patronage of the state.

ARTICLE XV: MILITIA

Section 1. Composition of Militia

The militia of the state of South Dakota shall consist of all able-bodied male persons residing in the state, between the ages of eighteen and forty-five years, except such persons as now are, or hereafter may be, exempted by the laws of the United States or of this state.

Section 2. Legislative Provisions for Militia

The Legislature shall provide by law for the enrollment, uniforming, equipment and discipline of the militia and the establishment of volunteer and such other organizations or both, as may be deemed necessary for the protection of the state, the preservation of order and the efficiency and good of the service.

Section 3. Conformity to Federal Regulations

The Legislature in providing for the organization of the militia shall conform, as nearly as practicable, to the regulations for the government of the armies of the United States.

Section 4. Commissions of Officers of Militia

All militia officers shall be commissioned by the Governor, and may hold their commissions for such period of time as the Legislature may provide, subject to removal by the Governor for cause, to be first ascertained by a court-martial pursuant to law.

Section 5. Militia Privileged from Arrest

The militia shall in cases except treason, felony or breach of the peace, be privileged from arrest during their attendance at muster and elections and in going to and returning from the same.

Section 6. Safekeeping of Military Records and Relics

All military records, banners and relics of the state, except when in lawful use, shall be preserved in the office of _the adjutant general as an enduring memorial of the patriotism and valor of South Dakota; and it shall be the duty of the Legislature to provide by law for the safekeeping of the same.

Section 7. Conscientious Objectors

No person having conscientious scruples against bearing arms shall be compelled to do military duty in time of peace.

ARTICLE XVI: IMPEACHMENT
AND REMOVAL FROM OFFICE

Section 1. Power of Impeachment in House – Majority Required

The house of representatives shall have the sole power of impeachment. The concurrence of a majority of all members elected shall be necessary to an impeachment.

Section 2. Trial of Impeachments – Presiding Officer

All impeachments shall be tried by the senate. When sitting for that purpose the senators shall be upon oath or affirmation to do justice according to law and evidence. No person shall be convicted without the concurrence of two-thirds of the members elected. When the Governor or lieutenant governor is on trial the presiding judge of the Supreme Court shall preside.

Section 3. Officers Subject to Impeachment – Grounds – Removal from Office – Criminal Prosecution

The Governor and other state and judicial officers, except county judges, justices of the peace and police magistrates, shall be liable to impeachment for drunkenness, crimes, corrupt conduct, or malfeasance or misdemeanor in office, but judgment in such cases shall not extend further than to removal from office and disqualification to hold any office of trust or profit under the state. The person accused whether convicted or acquitted shall nevertheless be liable to indictment, trial, judgment and punishment according to law.

Section 4. Removals of Officers not Subject to Impeachment

All officers not liable to impeachment shall be subject to removal for misconduct or malfeasance or crime or misdemeanor in office, or for drunkenness or gross incompetency, in such manner as may be provided by law.

Section 5. Suspension of Duties Between Impeachment and Acquittal

No officer shall exercise the duties of his office after he shall have been impeached and before his acquittal.

Section 6. Lieutenant Governor not to try Governor

On trial of an impeachment against the Governor the lieutenant governor shall not act as a member of the court.

Section 7. Service of Copy of Impeachment Before Trial Required

No person shall be tried on impeachment before he shall have been served with a copy thereof at least twenty days previous to the day set for trial.

Section 8. Impeachment Twice for Same Offense Prohibited

No person shall be liable to impeachment twice for the same offense.

ARTICLE XVII: CORPORATIONS

Section 1. Special Corporation Laws Prohibited – State-Controlled Corporations Excepted

No corporation shall be created or have its charter extended, changed or amended by special laws, except those for charitable, educational, penal or reformatory purposes, which are to be and remain under the patronage and control of the state; but the Legislature shall provide, by general laws, for the organization of all corporations hereafter to be created.

Section 2. Invalidation of Charters Without Bona Fide Organization and Business

All existing charters, or grants of special or exclusive privileges under which a bona fide organization shall not have taken place and business been commenced in good faith at the time this Constitution takes effect, shall thereafter have no validity.

Section 3. Laws for Benefit Of Corporation as Conditioned on Compliance with Constitutional Provision

The Legislature shall not remit the forfeiture of the charter of any corporation now existing nor alter or amend the same nor pass any other general or special law for the benefit of such corporation, except upon the condition that such corporation shall thereafter hold its charter subject to the provisions of this Constitution.

Section 4. Corporations Subject to Eminent Domain – Police Power

The exercise of the right of eminent domain shall never be abridged or so construed as to prevent the Legislature from taking the property and franchises of incorporated companies and subjecting them to public use, the same as the property of individuals; and the exercise of the police power of the state shall never be abridged or so construed as to permit corporations to conduct their business in such manner as to infringe the equal rights of individuals or the general well-being of the state.

Section 5. Casting of Votes for Directors or Managers

In all elections for directors or managers of a corporation, each member or shareholder may cast the whole number of his votes for one candidate, or distribute them upon two or more candidates, as he may prefer.

Section 6. Place of Business and Authorized Agent Required of Foreign Corporation

No foreign corporation shall do any business in this state without having one or more known places of business and an authorized agent or agents in the same upon whom process may be served.

Section 7. Business to be Expressed in Charter – Real Estate Restricted

No corporation shall engage in any business other than that expressly authorized in its charter, nor shall it take or hold any real estate except such as may be necessary and proper for its legitimate business.

Section 8. Stocks and Bonds – Indebtedness Increase

No corporation shall issue stocks or bonds except for money, labor done, or money or property actually received; and all fictitious increase of stock or indebtedness shall be void. The stock and indebtedness of corporations shall not be increased except in pursuance of general law, nor without the consent of the persons holding the larger amount in value of the stock first obtained, at a meeting to be held after sixty days' notice given in pursuance of law.

Section 9. Legislature's Power to Alter, Revise, or Annul Corporate Charters – Creation, Renewal, or Extension

The Legislature shall have the power to alter, revise or annul any charter of any corporation now existing and revocable at the taking effect of this Constitution, or any that may be created, whenever in their opinion it may be injurious to the citizens of this state, in such a manner, however, that no injustice shall be done to the incorporators. No law hereafter enacted shall create, renew or extend the charter of more than one corporation.

Section 10. Local Consent Required for Grant of Street Railroad Right

No law shall be passed by the Legislature granting the right to construct and operate a street railroad within any city, town or incorporated village, without requiring the consent of the local authorities having the control of the street or highway proposed to be occupied by such street railroad.

Section 11. Construction and Maintenance of Telegraph Lines – Controlling Interest in Competing Company Prohibited

Any association or corporation organized for the purpose, or any individual, shall have the right to construct and maintain lines of telegraph in this state and to connect the same with other lines; and the Legislature shall by general law of uniform operation provide reasonable regulations to give full effect to this section. No telegraph company shall consolidate with or hold a controlling interest in the stock or bonds of any other telegraph company owning a competing line, or acquire by purchase or otherwise, any other competing line of telegraph.

Section 12. Railroad Corporations

Every railroad corporation organized or doing business in this state under the laws or authority thereof shall have and maintain a public office or place in this state for the transaction of its business, where transfers of its stock shall be made, and in which shall be kept for public inspection books in which shall be recorded the amount of capital stock subscribed, and by whom; the names of the owners of its stock, and the amount owned by them respectively; the amount of stock paid in, and by whom; the transfers of said stock; the amount of its assets and liabilities; and the names and place of residence of its officers. The directors of every railroad corporation shall annually make a report, under oath, to the auditor of public accounts or some officer or officers to be designated by law, of all their acts and doings, which report shall include such matters relating to railroads as may be prescribed by law, and the Legislature shall pass laws enforcing by suitable penalties the provisions of this section.

Section 13. Movable Property of Railroad Corporation Considered Personality – Execution and Sale

The rolling stock, and all other movable property belonging to any railroad company or corporation in this state shall be considered personal property, and shall be liable to execution and sale in the same manner as the personal property of individuals, and the Legislature shall pass no laws exempting such property from execution and sale.

Section 14. Consolidation of Railroad Lines – Forfeiture of Charter for Evasion of Provisions

No railroad corporation shall consolidate its stock, property or franchises with any other railroad corporation owning a parallel or competing line; and in no case shall any consolidation take place except upon public notice given out, at least sixty days to all stockholders, in such manner as may be provided by law. Any attempt to evade the provisions of this section, by any railroad corporation, by lease or otherwise, shall work a forfeiture of its charter.

Section 15. Railways and Rail Companies Declared Public
Highways and Common Carriers – Regulation of Rates

Railways heretofore constructed or that may hereafter be
constructed, in this state are hereby declared public highways,
and all railroad and transportation companies are declared to be
common carriers and subject to legislative control; and the
Legislature shall have power to enact laws regulating and
controlling the rates of charges for the transportation of
passengers and freight as such common carriers from one point
to another in this state.

Section 16. Right to Construct and Operate Railroad –
Passengers, Tonnage and Cars

Any association or corporation organized for the purpose shall
have the right to construct and operate a railroad between any
points within this state, and to connect at the state line with
railroads of other states. Every railroad company shall have the
right with its road to intersect, connect with, or cross any other
railroad, and shall receive and transport each the other's
passengers, tonnage and cars, loaded or empty, without delay or
discrimination.

Section 17. Rate Discrimination Prevention

The Legislature shall pass laws to correct abuses and prevent
discrimination and extortion in the rates of freight and passenger
tariffs on the different railroads in this state, and enforce such
laws by adequate penalties, to the extent, if necessary for that
purpose, of forfeiture of their property and franchises.

Section 18. Compensation for Private Property Taken for Public
Use – Assessment of Damages

Municipal and other corporations and individuals invested with
the privilege of taking private property for public use shall make
just compensation for property taken, injured or destroyed, by

the construction or enlargement of their works, highways or improvements, which compensation shall be paid or secured before such taking, injury or destruction. The Legislature is hereby prohibited from depriving any person of an appeal from any preliminary assessment of damages against any such corporation or individuals made by viewers or otherwise; and the amount of such damages in all cases of appeal shall, on the demand of either party, be determined by a jury as in other civil cases.

Section 19. "Corporations" Defined

The term "corporations," as used in this article, shall be construed to include all joint stock companies or associations having any of the powers or privileges of corporations not possessed by individuals or partnerships.

Section 20. Monopolies and Trusts Prohibited-- Combinations in Restraint of Trade – Legislative Powers

Monopolies and trusts shall never be allowed in this state and no incorporated company, co-partnership or association of persons in this state shall directly or indirectly combine or make any contract with any incorporated company, foreign or domestic, through their stockholders or the trustees or assigns of such stockholders, or with any co-partnership or association of persons, or in any manner whatever to fix the prices, limit the production or regulate the transportation of any product or commodity so as to prevent competition in such prices, production or transportation or to establish excessive prices therefor. The Legislature shall pass laws for the enforcement of this section by adequate penalties and in the case of incorporated companies, if necessary for that purpose may, as a penalty, declare a forfeiture of their franchises.

Section 21. Corporate or Syndicate Farming Prohibited –
Definitions – Restrictions

No corporation or syndicate may acquire, or otherwise obtain an
interest, whether legal, beneficial, or otherwise, in any real
estate used for farming in this state, or engage in farming. The
term, corporation, means any corporation organized under the
laws of any state of the United States or any country. The term,
syndicate, includes any limited partnership, limited liability
partnership, business trust, or limited liability company organized
under the laws of any state of the United States or any country.
A syndicate does not include general partnerships, except
general partnerships in which non-family farm syndicates or non-
family farm corporations are partners. The term, farming, means
the cultivation of land for the production of agricultural crops,
fruit, or other horticultural products, or the ownership, keeping,
or feeding of animals for the production of livestock or livestock
products. Section 22. Restrictions – Application. The restrictions
in Section 21 of this Article do not apply to:

A family farm corporation or syndicate.

A family farm corporation or syndicate is a corporation or
syndicate engaged in farming or the ownership of agricultural
land, in which a majority of the partnership interests, shares,
stock, or other ownership interests are held by members of a
family or a trust created for the benefit of a member of that
family.

The term, family, means natural persons related to one another
within the fourth degree of kinship according to civil law, or their
spouses. At least one of the family members in a family farm
corporation or syndicate shall reside on or be actively engaged in
the day-to-day labor and management of the farm.

Day-to-day labor and management shall require both daily or

routine substantial physical exertion and administration.

(1) None of the corporation's or syndicate's partners, members, or stockholders may be nonresident aliens, or other corporations or syndicates, unless all of the stockholders, members, or partners of such entities are persons related within the fourth degree of kinship to the majority of partners, members, or stockholders in the family farm corporation or syndicate;

(2) Agricultural land acquired or leased, or livestock kept, fed or owned, by a cooperative organized under the laws of any state, if a majority of the shares or other interests of ownership in the cooperative are held by members in the cooperative who are natural persons actively engaged in the day-to-day labor and management of a farm, or family farm corporations or syndicates, and who either acquire from the cooperative, through purchase or otherwise, such livestock, or crops produced on such land, or deliver to the cooperative, through sale or otherwise, crops to be used in the keeping or feeding of such livestock;

(3) Nonprofit corporations organized under state non-profit corporation law;

(4) Agricultural land, which, as of the approval date of this amendment, is being farmed, or which is owned or leased, or in which there is a legal or beneficial interest, directly or indirectly owned, acquired, or obtained by a corporation or syndicate, if such land or other interest is held in continuous ownership or under continuous lease by the same such corporation or syndicate. For the purposes of this exemption, land purchased on a contract signed as of the approval date of this amendment is considered as owned on that date;

(5) Livestock, which as of the approval date of this amendment, is owned by a corporation or syndicate. For the purposes of this exemption, livestock to be produced under contract for a corporation or syndicate are considered as owned, if the contract is for the keeping or feeding of livestock and is signed as of the approval date of this amendment, and if the contract remains in effect and is not terminated by either party to the contract. This exemption does not extend beyond the term of any contract signed as of the approval date of this amendment;

(6) A farm operated for research or experimental purposes, if any commercial sales from the farm are only incidental to the research or experimental objectives of the corporation or syndicate;

(7) Land leases by alfalfa processors for the production of alfalfa;

(8) Agricultural land operated for the purpose of growing seed, nursery plants, or sod;

(9) Mineral rights on agricultural land;

(10) Agricultural land acquired or leased by a corporation or syndicate for immediate or potential non-farming purposes, for a period of five years from the date of purchase. A corporation or syndicate may hold such agricultural land in such acreage as may be necessary to its nonfarm business operation, but pending the development of the agricultural land for nonfarm purposes, such land may not be used for farming except under lease to a family farm corporation or family farm syndicate or a non-syndicate or non-corporate farm;

(11) Agricultural lands or livestock acquired by a corporation or syndicate by process of law in the collection of debts, or by any procedures for the enforcement of a lien, encumbrance, or claim thereon, whether created by mortgage or otherwise. Any lands so acquired shall be disposed of within a period of five years and may not be used for farming before being disposed of, except under a lease to a family farm corporation or syndicate, or a non-syndicate or non-corporate farm. Any livestock so acquired shall be disposed of within six months;

(12) Agricultural lands held by a state or nationally chartered bank as trustee for a person, corporation or syndicate that is otherwise exempt from the provisions of sections 21 to 24, inclusive, of this Article;

(13) A bona fide encumbrance taken for purposes of security;

(14) Custom spraying, fertilizing, or harvesting;

(15) Livestock futures contracts, livestock purchased for slaughter within two weeks of the purchase date, or livestock purchased and resold within two weeks.

Section 23. Loss of Qualification – Re-qualification or Dissolution

If a family farm corporation or family farm syndicate that has qualified under all the requirements of a family farm corporation or a family farm syndicate ceases to meet the defined criteria, it has twenty years, if the ownership of the majority of the stock of such corporation, or the majority of the ownership interest of such syndicate, continues to be held by persons related to one another within the fourth degree of kinship or their spouses, and their land holdings are not increased, to either re-qualify as a family farm corporation or family farm syndicate or dissolve and return to personal ownership.

Section 24. Annual Report – Violations – Action and Enforcement

Any corporation or syndicate that owns agricultural land or engages in farming is required to report information necessary for the enforcement of sections 21 to 24, inclusive, of this Article to the Secretary of State on an annual basis, under rules promulgated by the Secretary pursuant to state law.

The Secretary of State shall monitor such reports and notify the Attorney General of any possible violations, and any resident of the state may also notify the Attorney General of any possible violations.

If a corporation or syndicate violates any provision of sections 21 to 24, inclusive, of this Article, the Attorney General shall commence an action in circuit court to enjoin any pending illegal purchase of land or livestock, or to force divestiture of land or livestock held in violation of sections 21 to 24, inclusive, of this Article.

The court shall order any land held in violation of sections 21 to 24 of this Article to be divested within two years and any livestock to be divested within six months.

If land so ordered by the court has not been divested within two years, the court shall declare the land escheated to the state.

If the Attorney General fails to bring an action in circuit court to enforce sections 21 to 24, inclusive, of this Article, any resident of the state has standing in circuit court to sue for enforcement.

ARTICLE XVIII: BANKING AND CURRENCY

Section 1. General Banking Law – Provisions Required

If a general banking law shall be enacted it shall provide for the registry and countersigning by an officer of this state of all bills or paper credit designed to circulate as money, and require security to the full amount thereof, to be deposited with the state treasurer, in the approved securities of the state or of the United States, to be rated at ten per centum below their par value, and in case of their depreciation the deficiency shall be made good by depositing additional securities.

Section 2. Bank to Cease Operations Within Twenty Years of Organization – Reorganization

Every bank, banking company or corporation shall be required to cease all banking operations within twenty years from the time of its organization, and promptly thereafter close its business, but shall have corporate capacity to sue or be sued until its business is fully closed, but the Legislature may provide by general law for the reorganization of such banks.

Section 3. Liability of Banking Corporation Shareholders and Stockholders – Exemption Under Federal Law

The shareholders or stockholders of any banking corporation shall be held individually responsible and liable for all contracts, debts and engagements of such corporation to the extent of the amount of their stock therein, at the par value thereof, in addition to the amount invested in such shares or stock and such individual liability shall continue for one year after any transfer or sale of stock by any stockholder or stockholders. Provided that if the shareholders and stockholders of any national banking corporation shall be exempt from liability by federal law then and in that event the liability upon shareholders and stockholders of state banking corporations herein imposed shall not be operative in the event that such state banking corporation has membership in the federal deposit insurance corporation.

ARTICLE XIX: CONGRESSIONAL AND LEGISLATIVE APPORTIONMENT

Section 1. Congressional Representatives Elected at Large

Until otherwise provided by law, the members of the house of representatives of the United States, apportioned to this state, shall be elected by the state at large.

Section 2. Senatorial and Representative Districts – Apportionment

Omitted

ARTICLE XX: SEAT OF GOVERNMENT

Section 1. Temporary Seat of Government – Vote

The question of the location of the temporary seat of government shall be submitted to a vote of the electors of the proposed state of South Dakota in same manner and at the same election at which this Constitution shall be submitted, and the place receiving the highest number of votes shall be the temporary seat of government until a permanent seat of government shall be established as hereinafter provided.

Section 2. Permanent Seat of Government – Vote

The Legislature at its first session after the admission of this state, shall provide for the submission of the question of a place for a permanent seat of government to the qualified voters of the state at the next general election thereafter, and that place which receives a majority of all the votes cast upon that question shall be the permanent seat of government.

Section 3. Election Between Two Places with Highest Votes if Majority Vote not Received

Should no place voted for at said election have a majority of all votes cast upon this question, the Governor shall issue his proclamation for an election to be held in the same manner at the next general election to choose between the two places having received the highest number of votes cast at the first election on this question. This election shall be conducted in the same manner as the first election for the permanent seat of government, and the place receiving the majority of all votes cast upon this question shall be the permanent seat of government.

ARTICLE XXI: MISCELLANEOUS

Section 1. Seal and Coat of Arms

The design of the great seal of South Dakota shall be as follows: A circle within which shall appear in the left foreground a smelting furnace and other features of mining work. In the left background a range of hills. In the right foreground a farmer at his plow. In the right background a herd of cattle and a field of corn. Between the two parts thus described shall appear a river bearing a steamboat. Properly divided between the upper and lower edges of the circle shall appear the legend, "Under God the People Rule" which shall be the motto of the state of South Dakota. Exterior to this circle and within a circumscribed circle shall appear, in the upper part, the words, "State of South Dakota," in the lower part the words, "Great Seal," and the date in Arabic numerals of the year in which the state shall be admitted to the union.

Section 2. Salary of Constitutional Officers

The Legislature by two-thirds vote of each branch thereof at any regular session may fix the salary of any or all constitutional officers including members of the Legislature. In fixing any such salary the Legislature shall determine the effective date thereof and may in its discretion decrease or increase the salary of any officer during his term.

Section 3. Oath of Office

Every person elected or appointed to any office in this state, except such inferior offices as may be by law exempted, shall, before entering upon the duties thereof, take an oath or affirmation to support the Constitution of the United States and of this state, and faithfully to discharge the duties of his office.

Section 4. Exemptions

The right of the debtor to enjoy the comforts and necessaries of life shall be recognized by wholesome laws exempting from forced sale a homestead, the value of which shall be limited and defined by law, to all heads of families, and a reasonable amount of personal property, the kind and value of which to be fixed by general laws.

Section 5. Rights of Married Women

The real and personal property of any woman in this state, acquired before marriage, and all property to which she may after marriage become in any manner rightfully entitled, shall be her separate property, and shall not be liable for the debts of her husband.

Section 6. Drainage of Agricultural Lands

The drainage of agricultural lands is hereby declared to be a public purpose and the Legislature may provide therefor, and may provide for the organization of drainage districts for the drainage of lands for any public use, and may vest the corporate authorities thereof, and the corporate authorities of counties, townships and municipalities, with power to construct levees, drains and ditches, and to keep in repair all drains, ditches and levees heretofore constructed under the laws of this state, by special assessments upon the property benefited thereby, according to benefits received.

Section 7. Irrigation of Agricultural Lands

The irrigation of agricultural lands is hereby declared to be a public purpose and the Legislature may provide for the organization of irrigation districts for the irrigation of land, and may vest the corporate authorities thereof and the corporate authorities of counties, townships and municipalities with the power to construct, operate and maintain irrigation dams, reservoirs, canals, flumes, ditches and laterals, and to keep in repair all irrigation dams, reservoirs, canals, flumes, ditches and laterals heretofore constructed, under the laws of the state, by special assessments upon the property benefited thereby, according to the benefits received.

Section 8. Hail Insurance

The providing of insurance against loss or damage to crops by hail is hereby declared to be a public purpose, and the Legislature is authorized and empowered to levy an assessment upon agricultural land for such purpose, with such exemptions as may be provided by law. The state may be divided into hail insurance districts and the assessment per acre in the different districts shall be as the Legislature may determine, but such assessment shall be uniform upon all land of the same district that is similarly situated. The assessment hereby authorized may be levied by the Legislature direct, or by the corporate authorities of the districts herein provided for, or by such other agency as may be authorized by general law.

Section 9. Marriage

Only marriage between a man and a woman shall be valid or recognized in South Dakota. The uniting of two or more persons in a civil union, domestic partnership, or other quasi-marital relationship shall not be valid or recognized in South Dakota.

ARTICLE XXII: COMPACT WITH THE UNITED STATES

Section 1:

The following article shall be irrevocable without the consent of the United States and the people of the state of South Dakota expressed by their legislative assembly: First. That perfect toleration of religious sentiment shall be secured, and that no inhabitant of this state shall ever be molested in person or property on account of his or her mode of religious worship. Second. That we, the people inhabiting the state of South Dakota, do agree and declare that we forever disclaim all right and title to the unappropriated public lands lying within the boundary of South Dakota, and to all lands lying within said limits owned or held by any Indian or Indian tribes; and that until the title thereto shall have been extinguished by the United States, the same shall be and remain subject to the disposition of the United States; and said Indian lands shall remain under the absolute jurisdiction and control of the Congress of the United States; that the lands belonging to citizens of the United States residing without the said state shall never be taxed at a higher rate than the lands belonging to residents of this state; that no taxes shall be imposed by the state of South Dakota on lands or property therein belonging to or which may hereafter be purchased by the United States, or reserved for its use. But nothing herein shall preclude the state of South Dakota from taxing as other lands are taxed any lands owned or held by any Indian who has severed his tribal relation and has obtained from the United States, or from any person a title thereto by patent or other grant save and except such lands as have been or may be granted to any Indian or Indians under any act of Congress containing a provision exempting the lands thus granted from taxation. All such lands which may have been exempted by any grant or law of the United States, shall remain exempt to the extent, and as prescribed by such act of Congress. Third. That the state of South Dakota shall assume and pay that portion of the debts and liabilities of the territory of Dakota as provided in this Constitution. Fourth. That provision shall be made for the establishment and maintenance of systems of public schools, which shall be open to all the children of this state, and free from sectarian control.

ARTICLE XXIII AMENDMENTS AND REVISIONS OF THE CONSTITUTION

Section 1. Amendments

Amendments to this Constitution may be proposed by initiative or by a majority vote of all members of each house of the Legislature. An amendment proposed by initiative shall require a petition signed by qualified voters equal in number to at least ten percent of the total votes cast for Governor in the last gubernatorial election. The petition containing the text of the proposed amendment and the names and addresses of its sponsors shall be filed at least one year before the next general election at which the proposed amendment is submitted to the voters. A proposed amendment may amend one or more articles and related subject matter in other articles as necessary to accomplish the objectives of the amendment.

Section 2. Revision

A convention to revise this Constitution may be called by a three-fourths vote of all the members of each house. The calling of a constitutional convention may be initiated and submitted to the voters in the same manner as an amendment. If a majority of the voters voting thereon approve the calling of a convention, the Legislature shall provide for the holding thereof. Members of a convention shall be elected on a nonpolitical ballot in the same districts and in the same number as the House of Representatives. Proposed amendments or revisions approved by a majority of all the members of the convention shall be submitted to the electorate at a special election in a manner to be determined by the convention.

Section 3. Ratification

Any constitutional amendment or revision must be submitted to the voters and shall become a part of the Constitution only when approved by a majority of the votes cast thereon. The Legislature may provide for the withdrawal by its sponsors of an initiated amendment at any time prior to its submission to the voters.

ARTICLE XXIV: PROHIBITION

Repealed

ARTICLE XXV: MINORITY REPRESENTATION

Rejected

ARTICLE XXVI: SCHEDULE AND ORDINANCE

Section 1. Continuation of Prior Writs, Actions, Claims, and Bodies Corporate – Validation of Previously Issued Process

That no inconvenience may arise from the change of the territorial government to the permanent state government, it is hereby declared that all writs, actions, prosecutions, claims and rights of individuals, and all bodies corporate, shall continue as if no change had taken place in this government; and all process which may be before the organization of the judicial department, under this Constitution, issued under the authority of the territory of Dakota, within the boundary of this state, shall be as valid as if issued in the name of the state of South Dakota.

Section 2. Fines, Forfeitures and Escheats of Territory to Accrue to State

That all fines, penalties, forfeitures and escheats accruing to the territory of Dakota, within the boundary of the state of South Dakota, shall accrue to the use of said state.

Section 3. Recognizances, Bonds, Obligations and Undertakings – Criminal Prosecutions and Penal Actions

That all recognizances, bonds, obligations or other undertakings, heretofore taken, or which may be taken before the organization of the judicial department under this Constitution, shall remain valid, and shall pass over to, and may be prosecuted in the name of the state of South Dakota; and all bonds, obligations or undertakings, executed to this territory, within the boundaries of the state of South Dakota, or to any officer in his official capacity, shall pass over to the proper state authority, and to their successors in office, for the uses therein respectively expressed, and may be sued for and recovered accordingly. All criminal prosecutions and penal actions, which have arisen, or which may arise before the organization of the judicial department under this Constitution, and which shall then be pending, may be prosecuted to judgment and executed in the name of the state.

Section 4. Civil and Military Officers

All officers, civil and military, now holding their offices and appointments in this territory under the authority of the United States, or under the authority of the territory of Dakota, shall continue to hold and exercise their respective offices and appointments until superseded under this Constitution: provided, that the provisions of the above sections shall be subject to the provisions of the act of Congress providing for the admission of the state of South Dakota, approved by the president of the United States on February 22, 1889.

Section 5. Election of Constitution and State Officers – Ballots

This Constitution shall be submitted for adoption or rejection to a vote of the electors qualified by the laws of this territory to vote at all elections, at the election to be held on Tuesday, October 1, 1889. At the said election the ballots shall be in the following form: For the Constitution: Yes. No. For prohibition: Yes. No. For minority representation: Yes. No. As a heading to each of said ballots shall be printed on each ballot the following instructions to voters: All persons desiring to vote for the Constitution, or for any of the articles submitted to a separate vote, must erase the word "No." All persons who desire to vote against the Constitution, or against any article submitted separately, must erase the word "Yes." Any person may have printed or written on his ballot only the words "for the Constitution," or "against the Constitution," and such ballot shall be counted for or against the Constitution accordingly. The same provision shall apply to articles submitted separately. In addition to the foregoing election for the Constitution and for the articles submitted by this convention for a separate vote thereon, an election shall be held at the same time and places, by the said qualified electors, for the following state officers, to be voted for on the same ballot as above provided for votes on the Constitution and separate articles, to wit: A Governor, lieutenant governor, secretary of state, auditor, treasurer, attorney general, superintendent of public instruction, commissioner of school and public lands, judges of the Supreme, circuit and county Courts, representatives in Congress, state senators, and representatives in the Legislature. All the elections above provided for shall be held in the same manner and form as provided for the election for the adoption or rejection of the Constitution. And the names of all the officers above specified to be voted for at such election shall be written or printed upon the same ballots as the vote for or against the Constitution. The judges of election in counting the ballots voted at such election shall count all the affirmative ballots upon the Constitution as votes for the Constitution; and they shall count all the negative ballots voted at said election upon the Constitution as votes against the Constitution; and ballots voted at said election upon which neither of said words "yes" or "no" following the words "for the Constitution" are erased, shall not be counted upon such proposition. And they shall count all affirmative ballots so voted upon the article on prohibition separately submitted, as votes for such article, and they shall count all negative ballots so voted upon such article as votes against such article; and ballots upon which neither the words "yes" or "no" following the words "for prohibition" are erased, shall not be counted upon such proposition; and they shall count all the affirmative ballots so voted upon the article on minority representation, separately submitted, as votes for such article. And they shall count all negative ballots so voted upon such article as votes against such article; and ballots upon which neither of said words "yes" or "no" following the words "for minority representation" are erased, shall not be counted upon such proposition. If it shall appear in accordance with the returns hereinafter provided for, that a majority of the votes polled at such election, for and against the Constitution, are for the Constitution, then this Constitution shall be the Constitution of the state of South Dakota. If it shall appear, according to the returns hereinafter provided for, that a majority of all votes cast at said election for and against "prohibition" are for prohibition then said article XIV shall be and form a part of this Constitution, and be in full force and effect as such from date of said election, but if a majority of said votes shall appear, according to said returns to be against prohibition, then article XXIV shall be null and void and shall not be a part of this Constitution. And if it appear, according to the returns hereinafter provided for, that a majority of all votes cast at said election for and against "minority representation" are for minority representation, then article XXV shall be and form a part of said Constitution, and be in full force and effect as such from the date of said election; but if a majority of said votes shall appear, according to said returns, to be against minority representation, then said article XXV shall be null and void and shall not be a part of this Constitution. At such election the person voted for, for any one of the offices to be filled at such election, who shall receive the highest number of votes cast at said election, shall be declared elected to said office.

Section 6. Election for Temporary Seat of Government

At the same time and places of election there shall be held by said qualified electors an election for the place of the temporary seat of government. On each ballot, and on the same ballot on which are the matters voted for or against, as hereinbefore provided, shall be written or printed the words "for temporary seat of government," (Here insert the name of the city, town or place, to be voted for.) And upon the canvass and return of the vote, made as hereinafter provided for, the name of the city, town or place which shall have received the largest number of votes for said temporary seat of government, shall be declared by the Governor, chief justice and secretary of the territory of Dakota, or by any two of them, at the same time that they shall canvass the vote for or against the Constitution, together with the whole number of votes cast for each city, town or place, and the officers above named, shall immediately after the result of said election shall have been ascertained, issue a proclamation directing the Legislature elected at said election to assemble at said city, town or place so selected, on the day fixed by this schedule and ordinance.

Section 7. Conduct of Election

The election provided for herein shall be under the provisions of the Constitution herewith submitted, and shall be conducted in all respects as elections are conducted under the general laws of the territory of Dakota, except as herein provided. No mere technicalities or informalities in the manner or form of election, or neglect of any officer to perform his duty with regard thereto, shall be deemed to vitiate or avoid the same, it being the true intent and object of this ordinance to ascertain and give effect to the true will of the people of the state of South Dakota, as expressed by their votes at the polls.

Section 8. Election Returns

Immediately after the election herein provided for, the judges of election at each voting place shall make a true and complete count of all the votes duly cast at such election, and shall certify and return the result of the same, with the names of all the candidates and the number of votes cast for each candidate, and the number of votes cast for and against the Constitution, and the number of votes cast for and against prohibition, and the number of votes cast for and against minority representation, and the number of votes cast for each city, town or place for the "temporary seat of government," to the county clerk, or auditor of the respective counties, together with one of the poll lists and election books used in said election.

Section 9. Canvass of Vote – Filing with County Clerks or Auditors

Within five days after said election the several boards of county canvassers provided by law for the canvassing of the results of the election, shall make and certify to the secretary of the territory of Dakota the true and correct return of the total number of votes cast for the Constitution, and against the Constitution, of the number of votes cast for and against "prohibition," and the number of votes cast for and against "minority representation," and the number of votes cast for each city, town or place as the "temporary seat of government," and of the number of votes cast for each person voted for at such election, except county officers and members of the Legislature, and shall transmit the same to the secretary of the territory of Dakota, by mail, and shall file with the county clerk or auditor of each of said counties a duplicate and certified copy of said return. Said board of county canvassers shall issue certificates of election to the persons who shall have received the highest number of votes cast for the respective offices of judge of the county court, and representatives in the Legislature, and for state senator or senators.

Section 10. Certification of Senator or Representative from Multi-County District

When two or more counties are connected in one senatorial or representative district, it shall be the duty of the clerks and auditors of the respective counties to attend at the office of the county clerk of the senior county in the date of organization within twenty days after the date of election, and they shall compare the votes given in the several counties comprising such senatorial and representative district and such clerks or auditors shall immediately make out a certificate of election to the person having the highest number of votes in such district for state senator or representative or both; which certificate shall be delivered to the person entitled thereto on his application to the clerk of the senior county of such district.

Section 11. Delivery of Returns to Proper State Officer – Certification to President – Proclamation of Election Result – Lists of Elected Officers – Certificates of Election

The secretary of the territory shall receive all returns of election transmitted to him as above provided, and shall preserve the same, and after they have been canvassed as hereinafter provided, and after the admission of the state of South Dakota into the union, he shall deliver said returns to the proper state officer of said state of South Dakota. Within fifteen days after said election the secretary of the territory, with the Governor and chief justice thereof, or any two of them, shall canvass such returns and certify the same to the president of the United States, as provided in the Enabling Act. They shall also ascertain the total number of votes cast at such election for the Constitution and against the Constitution; the total number of votes cast for and against prohibition; and the total number of votes cast for and against minority representation; and the total number of votes cast for each city, town or place as the "temporary seat of government"; and the total number of votes cast for each person voted for, for any office at said election, excepting county judges and members of the Legislature, and shall declare the result of said election in conformity with such vote, and the Governor of the territory shall thereupon issue a proclamation at once thereof. They shall also make and transmit to the state Legislature, immediately upon its organization, a list of all the state and judicial officers who shall thus be ascertained to be duly elected. The various county and district canvassing boards shall make and transmit to the secretary of the territory the names of all persons declared by them to be elected members of the senate and house of representatives of the state of South Dakota; he shall make separate lists of the senators and representatives so elected, which list shall constitute the rolls under which the senate and house of representatives shall be organized. The Governor of the territory shall make and issue certificates of election to the persons who are shown by the canvass to have received the highest number of votes for Governor, lieutenant governor, secretary of state, auditor, treasurer, attorney general, superintendent of public instruction, commissioner of school and public lands and judges of the Supreme and circuit Courts. Such certificates to be attested by the secretary of the territory.

Section 12. Apportionment of State Legislature – Number of Senators and Representatives Initially Elected

The apportionment made in this Constitution shall govern the elections above provided for members of the state Legislature, until otherwise provided by law. At the first election held under this ordinance for senators and representatives of the Legislature, there shall be elected forty-five senators and one hundred and twenty-four representatives in the state Legislature respectively.

Section 13. First Assembly of Legislature – Oaths of Office

The Legislature elected under the provisions of this ordinance and Constitution shall assemble at the temporary seat of government on the third Tuesday in October, in the year A. D. 1889, at 12 o'clock noon, and on the first day of their assemblage the Governor and other state officers shall take the oath of office in the presence of the Legislature. The oath of office shall be administered to the members of the Legislature and to the state officers by the chief justice of the territory, or by any other officer duly authorized by the laws of the territory of Dakota to administer oaths.

Section 14. Election of Two United States Senators – Two Representatives

Immediately after the organization of the Legislature and taking the oath of office by the state officers, the Legislature shall then and there proceed to the election of two senators of the United States for the state of South Dakota, in the mode and manner provided by the laws of Congress for the election of United States senators. And the Governor and the secretary of the state of South Dakota shall certify the election of the said senators and two representatives in Congress, in the manner required by law.

Section 15. Adjournment After Election of Senators – Next
Meeting

Immediately after the election of the United States senators as
above provided for, said Legislature shall adjourn to meet at the
temporary seat of government on the first Tuesday after the first
Monday of January, 1890, at 12 o'clock m.; provided, however,
that if the state of South Dakota has not been admitted by
proclamation or otherwise at said date, then said Legislature
shall convene within ten days after the date of the admission of
the state into the union.

Section 16. Legislature and Officers to Exercise Necessary and
Authorized Powers only Pending Admission of State into Union

Nothing in this Constitution or schedule contained shall be
construed to authorize the Legislature to exercise any powers
except such as are necessary to its first organization, and to elect
United States senators, and to adjourn as above provided. Nor to
authorize any officer of the executive, administrative or judiciary
departments to exercise any duties of his office until the state of
South Dakota shall have been regularly admitted into the union,
accepting such as may be authorized by the Congress of the
United States.

Section 17. Validity of Ordinances and Schedule

The ordinances and schedule enacted by this convention shall be
held to be valid for all the purposes thereof.

Section 18. Freedom of Religion – Public Lands – Indian Lands
– Uniformity of Taxation – Territorial Debt – Public Schools –
Federal Reservations – Irrevocability

That we, the people of the state of South Dakota, do ordain:

First: That perfect toleration of religious sentiment shall be secured, and that no inhabitant of this state shall ever be molested in person or property on account of his or her mode of religious worship.

Second: That we, the people inhabiting the state of South Dakota, do agree and declare, that we forever disclaim all right and title to the unappropriated public lands lying within the boundaries of South Dakota; and to all lands lying within said limits owned or held by any Indian or Indian tribes, and that until the title thereto shall have been extinguished by the United States the same shall be and remain subject to the disposition of the United States, and said Indian lands shall remain under the absolute jurisdiction and control of the Congress of the United States; that the lands belonging to citizens of the United States residing without the said state, shall never be taxed at a higher rate than the lands belonging to residents of this state. That no taxes shall be imposed by the state of South Dakota on lands or property therein belonging to or which may hereafter be purchased by the United States, or reserved for its use. But nothing herein shall preclude the state of South Dakota from taxing as other lands are taxed any lands owned or held by any Indian who has severed his tribal relation and has obtained from the United States, or from any person a title thereto by patent or other grant save and except such lands _as have been, or may be granted to any Indian or Indians under any act of Congress containing a provision exempting the lands thus granted from taxation, all such lands which may have been exempted by any grant or law of the United States, shall remain exempt to the extent, and as prescribed by such act of Congress.

Third: That the state of South Dakota shall assume and pay that portion of the debts and liabilities of the territory of Dakota as provided in this Constitution.

Fourth: That provision shall be made for the establishment and maintenance of systems of public schools, which shall be open to all the children of this state, and free from sectarian control.

Fifth: That jurisdiction is ceded to the United States over the military reservations of Fort Meade, Fort Randall and Fort Sully, heretofore declared by the president of the United States: provided legal process, civil and criminal, of this state shall extend over such reservations, in all cases of which exclusive jurisdiction is not vested in the United States, or of crimes not committed within the limits of such reservations.

These ordinances shall be irrevocable without the consent of the United States, and also the people of the said state of South Dakota, expressed by their legislative assembly.

Section 19. Tenure of Elected Officers

The tenure of all officers, whose election is provided for in this schedule, on the first day of October, A. D. 1889, shall be as follows: The Governor, lieutenant governor, secretary of state, auditor, treasurer, attorney general, superintendent of public instruction, commissioner of school and public lands, judges of county courts, shall hold their respective offices until the first Tuesday, after the first Monday, in January, A. D. 1891, at twelve o'clock m., and until their successors are elected and qualified. The judges of the Supreme Court and circuit courts shall hold their offices until the first Tuesday, after the first Monday, in January, A. D. 1894, at twelve o'clock m., and until their successors are elected and qualified; subject to the provisions of Section 26 of article V of the Constitution. The terms of office of the members of the Legislature, elected at the first election held under the provisions of this Constitution, shall expire on the first Tuesday, after the first Monday, in January, 1891.

Section 20. Time of General Election

That the first general election under the provisions of this Constitution shall be held on the first Tuesday after the first Monday in November, 1890, and every two years thereafter. 79

Section 21. Form of Ballot

The following form of ballot is adopted: Constitutional Ticket INSTRUCTIONS TO VOTERS

All persons desiring to vote for the Constitution, or for any of the articles submitted to a separate vote, may erase the word "No." All persons who desire to vote against the Constitution, or any articles separately submitted may erase the word "Yes." For the Constitution: Yes. No. For Prohibition: Yes. No. For Minority Representation: Yes. No. For _____ as the temporary seat of government. For Governor.

_____

_ For Lieutenant Governor.

_____

_ For Secretary of State.

_____

_ For Auditor.

_____

_ For Treasurer.

_____

_ For Attorney General.

_____

_ For Superintendent of Public Instruction.

_____

_ For Commissioner of School and Public Lands.

_____

_ For Judges of the Supreme Court. First District_____
Second District_____ Third District_____ For

Judge of the Circuit Court ____ Circuit. For Representatives in Congress.

_____

_ For State Senator.

_____

_ For Representative in the Legislature.

_____

_ For County Judge.

_____

_

Section 22. Enrollment of Constitution – Delivery to Secretary of State – Inclusion in State Laws – Copy to President of United States

This Constitution shall be enrolled and after adoption and signing by the convention shall be delivered to Hon. A. J. Edgerton, the president of the constitutional convention, for safekeeping, and by him to be delivered to the secretary of state as soon as he assumes the duties of his office, and printed copies thereof shall be prefixed to the books containing the laws of the state and all future editions thereof. The president of this convention shall also supervise the making of the copy that must be sent to the president of the United States; said copy is to be certified by the president and chief clerk of this convention.

Section 23. Agreement by Joint Commission Concerning Territorial Records, Books, and Archives

The agreement made by the joint commission of the constitutional conventions of North and South Dakota concerning the records, books, and archives of the territory of Dakota is hereby ratified and confirmed, which agreement is in the words following: That is to say: The following books, records and archives of the territory of Dakota shall be the property of North Dakota, to wit: All records, books and archives in the offices of the Governor and secretary of the territory (except records of articles of incorporation of domestic corporations, returns of election of delegates to the constitutional convention of 1889, for South Dakota, returns of elections held under the so-called local option law in counties within the limits of South Dakota, bonds of notaries public appointed for counties within the limits of South Dakota, papers relating to the organization of counties situate within the limits of South Dakota, all of which records and archives are a part of the records and archives of said secretary's office; excepting also census returns from counties situate within the limits of South Dakota and papers relating to requisitions issued upon the application of officers of counties situate within the limits of South Dakota, all which are part of the records and archives of said Governor's office.) And the following records, books and archives shall also be the property of the state of North Dakota, to wit: Vouchers in the office or in the custody of the auditor of this territory relating to expenditures on account of public institutions, grounds or buildings situate within the limits of North Dakota; one warrant register in the office of the treasurer of this territory, being a record of warrants issued under and by virtue of chapter twenty-four of the laws enacted by the eighteenth legislative assembly of Dakota territory; all letters, receipts and vouchers in the same office now filed by counties and pertaining to counties within the limits of North Dakota; paid and canceled coupons in the same office representing interest on bonds which said state of North Dakota is to assume and pay; reports of gross earnings of the year 1888 in the same office, made by corporations operating lines of railroad situated wholly or mainly within the limits of North Dakota; records and papers of the office of the public examiner of the second district of the territory; records and papers of the office of the second district board of agriculture; records and papers in the office of the board of pharmacy of the district of North Dakota. All records, books and archives of the territory of Dakota which it is not herein agreed shall be the property of North Dakota, shall be the property of South Dakota. The following books shall be copied and the copies shall be the property of North Dakota, and the cost of such copies shall be borne equally by the said states of North Dakota and South Dakota. That is to say: Appropriation ledger for the years ending

November, 1889 and 1890 – one volume. The current warrant auditor's register – one volume. Insurance record for 1889 – one volume. Treasurer's cash book "D." Assessment ledger "B." Dakota territory bond register – one volume. Treasurer's current ledger – one volume. The originals of the foregoing volumes which are to be copied, shall at any time after such copying shall have been completed, be delivered on demand to the proper authorities of the state of South Dakota. All other records, books and archives which it is hereby agreed shall be the property of South Dakota shall remain at the capital of North Dakota until demanded by the Legislature of the state of South Dakota, and until the state of North Dakota shall have had a reasonable time after such demand is made to provide copies or abstracts or such portions thereof as the said state of North Dakota may desire to have copies or abstracts of. The state of South Dakota may also provide copies or abstracts of such records, books and archives which is agreed shall be the property of North Dakota as said state of South Dakota shall desire to have copies or abstracts of. The expense of all copies or abstracts of records, books and archives which it is herein agreed may be made, shall be borne equally by said two states.

ARTICLE XXVII: STATE CONTROL OF MANUFACTURE AND SALE OF LIQUOR

Repealed

ARTICLE XXVIII: COUNTY INVESTMENT OF PERMANENT SCHOOL AND INVESTMENT FUNDS

Section 1. School and Governmental Bonds – Farm Loans

The several counties of the state shall invest the moneys of the permanent school and endowment funds in bonds of school corporations, state, county and municipal bonds or in first mortgages upon good improved farm lands within their limits respectively, under such regulations as the Legislature may provide, but no farm loan shall exceed one thousand dollars to any one person, firm or corporation.

ARTICLE XXIX: STATE ELEVATORS, WAREHOUSES, FLOURING MILLS AND PACKING HOUSES

Section 1. Provision for Elevators and Warehouses – Marketing of Agricultural Products – Flouring Mills and Packing Houses

The Legislature may provide by law and appropriate money for the purchase or construction and operation of elevators and warehouses, within or without the state, for the marketing of agricultural products; and provided, further, that the Legislature may provide by law and appropriate money to buy or construct and operate flouring mills and packing houses within the state, if, in the future, and in the judgment of the Legislature, the public necessities may so require.

www.ingramcontent.com/pod-product-compliance
Lightning Source LLC
Chambersburg PA
CBHW071313220526

45468CB00001B/351